BURNING BRIDGES TO LIGHT THE WAY

ISBN 978-0-578-59846-8 Code 242J29
Burning Bridges to Light the Way

www.27bslash6.com

By the same author:

The Internet is a Playground
The *New York Times* bestselling first release by David Thorne featuring articles from 27bslash6 plus over 160 pages of new material.

I'll Go Home Then; It's Warm and Has Chairs
The second collection of all new essays and emails.

Look Evelyn, Duck Dynasty Wiper Blades, We Should Get Them
The third collection of new essays and emails.

That's Not How You Wash a Squirrel
The fourth collection of new essays and emails.

Wrap It In a Bit of Cheese Like You're Tricking the Dog
The fifth collection of new essays and emails.

Walk It Off, Princess
The sixth collection of new essays and emails.

Burning Bridges to Light the Way
You're holding it.

OFFICE MEMO PRESS

Not for Holly or Seb

Alternate Titles for This Book

That's Not Ben, It's a Very Thin Baby

The Vaper's Guide to the Samsung Galaxy

I Can't Today, I Have Shin Splints

Let's Go Fishing! A Guide for Young Anglers

Sebastian's Salt & Vinegar Bed Sheets

Beat Street 3: More Dancing, More Graffiti

I Had a Terrible Time, Fuck You

Découpage for Middle-Aged Women Named Carol

No Rules, Just Snakes

Legal Obligations When Trimming a Neighbour's Hedge

These Aren't My Arms

Harry Potter and the Avocado Dip

Lori Told Me Heather Never Cleans Her House

Staple Frittata and Other Dangerous Recipes

Reviews

"Just so you know, this isn't burning a bridge, this is declaring war. I did not give you permission to use my full name or write about putting golf balls in my anus. I'm meeting with my lawyer Thursday so expect to hear from them shortly. You fucked with the wrong person this time dipshit."

Wayne Redding

"I read the first chapter of your book last night. Watch your back loser. It will be when you least expect it. They weren't even my sister's underwear, they were my cousins."

Ray Paley

"No, I'm not cross about the stuff you wrote about me. Why would I be? I couldn't care less. It's not like you have a lot of readers. Joseph was a bit cross though. We've decided that we are going to write our own article about you. Your fans deserve to know the truth. We're going to write about the time you took Adderall for the first time at last year's SVBA event and asked Billy Robinson if he has Down's Syndrome then drove your car into a ravine."

Lori Snell

"Why did you write that I was arrested for shoplifting from Sephora in your book? I don't want everyone to know about that. You really are a cunt. I'm glad I spat in your coffee now. Like at least 20 times over the last few years."

Melissa Peters

"Thanks for the book. I run out toilet paper and used your book to wipe my ass. Sorry your funiture is uncomtable and ugly. We cant all have good tates."

Ian King

"Of course I'm annoyed. You said I never move and described me as a human sized slug but with more mucus and less ambition. I'm having a chilli cookoff at my house next Saturday and you're not invited. Sad to be you."

Cody Harenech

"I've spent the morning searching for your book online and leaving bad reviews. I've written over 10 so far. Hope it costs you a lot of money in sales. Payback's a bitch isn't it? And FYI, I wasn't masturbating while watching Lazy Town. My hands were dry and I was rubbing lotion on them and then I had an itch on the inside of my leg. I wasn't even watching Lazy Town, it was a Cooking By the Book Lil Jon remix on YouTube."

Ben Townsend

"Yes, I received the book. Please do not send anything to my parent's address again. I read the pages marked with sticky notes and then threw it out. I don't appreciate your juvenile comments about my faith or being referred to as Shitpants Sally and I could have died that day. That's something you would have had to live with for the rest of your life. I will pray for you."

Sally Mclaughlin

"I've never had sex with a homeless woman behind a dumpster in my life. How is that even funny? It's not. It just comes off as you being jealous of my exciting sex life."

Mark Shapiro

"Laugh it up funnyboy. You won't be laughing when I snap your skinny neck with a karate chop."

Gary Wright

"Not cool. The one thing I asked was that you don't mention drugs. That entire story is about taking drugs and you said that I fucked a fat girl. She wasn't fat. I told my dad that you made the entire thing up except the part about him hitting you with the television aerial. He says you're banned from his house for the rest of your life and he's going to email you an invoice for the ceramic rooster."

Thomas Harrer

"Our wedding wasn't Harry Potter themed you fucking liar. It was Magic Under the Stars. There was only one wand to open the ring box. Guests didn't have to bring their own wands. Why do you make this shit up? Also, there's no such superhero as Dark Wing."

Brandon Evans

"I'm not going to read your stupid shit. You still owe me $15 and a chainsaw asshole."

Clarence Shillinger

Contents

Foreword

By Peter Goers

There's a line, quite early in this book, that states, *"I get that some of the stuff I've written could be considered humiliating, but perhaps don't provide the content."*

It's important to remember this line as you wade through Thorne's barely coherent rants about friends, family, and colleagues. It's the line that may keep him from being sued, and apparently his excuse for being a dreadful human being.

Perhaps that's a little harsh. David isn't a dreadful human being all of the time. He has to sleep and I know he cares a lot about squirrels. There are parts of this book that even hint at a certain degree of empathy for other human beings. Some human beings, not all of them, maybe three. I once asked David if he's autistic and he replied, "It's pronounced *artistic* and no, not really. I can draw a cat though."

I assume he was joking but it's hard to tell with David. He once told me his grandfather was eaten by ants during an entomology expedition to Borneo. It was early in our friendship and I had no reason to believe this story wasn't true. David mentioned his grandfather a few years later and, when I asked if it was the same grandfather who had died in Borneo, he told me had made the story up about the ants, because he thought it was funny, and that his grandfather actually died in a windsurfing accident.

I first met David ten years ago, at a Japanese restaurant overlooking Adelaide's River Torrens. Earlier that morning, while waiting for my first studio guest to arrive, I leafed through a copy of *Wired Magazine* and came across an article David had written about time travel. The article, which likened gravitational time dilation to playing table tennis with cheese, was both informative and funny. I emailed David to let him know I'd enjoyed the article, and he replied within a few minutes with, "Thanks, sunshine. What are you doing for lunch?"

Perhaps he was just on his best behaviour that day, or maybe I was in an unusually good mood, but I found him to be quite amicable in real life. His online persona, particularly in regards to his website 27B/6, is that of a scoundrel, a polite scoundrel for the most part, but still a scoundrel. It's the role David is known for - his first book *The Internet is a Playground* was essentially just articles taken from the website - but many readers may be surprised to learn David also writes for several different publications under several pseudonyms.

His recent article about the North American River Otter in *National Geographic*, for example, displays not only the humour he is known for, but a rich knowledge and love of otters. His interviews and reviews for *Popular Mechanics* show an in-depth understanding of AI technologies, and his regular contributions to *Better Homes & Gardens* give a glimpse into David's favourite pastime - landscaping. His essay titled *Japanese Maples & Pea Gravel* was one of BH&G's most popular articles of 2019.

David is best known for his viral emails however, such as attempting to pay a bill with a drawing of a spider and ordering concrete from a florist, so it's interesting that this book, his 7th, contains very little in the way of email exchanges. Some of his long-time readers may be disappointed by this fact, others might appreciate the additional narrative. Without email headers taking up half the book, there's certainly more content.

Is it good content? Well, much of this book reads like the transcript of a drunk uncle telling an inappropriate story at a family function, but there are moments of cleverness, moments of reflection, and moments that will cause the reader to question if shelling out US$24.95 was a wise financial decision. With the Australian dollar at its current rate, this book costs nearly eighty dollars with postage and handling. That's forty dollars per chuckle.

It's difficult to define David's writing style but 'effortless' seems appropriate. It's as if he puts no effort into it whatsoever. There's no doubt a point hidden somewhere in the irreverent tangents and inside jokes, but he doesn't seem to care if you find it. Maybe that's the point. If so, it's not a very good one. As for the inside jokes, I suspect the only person who gets them is David. Take page 192 for example; a conversation that takes place in a comic book shop between two individuals named Brandon and Cody. No context is given, the two simply greet, discuss vaping, and say goodbye. Who are these people and why should anyone care if Cody's atomizer heads need rebuilding? A punchline that only the teller gets isn't a punchline, it's a sentence. Likely a run-on sentence in David's case. I suspect he just bashes away at the keyboard until he's distracted by a squirrel outside his window or it's time for a cigarette break. Perhaps that's the best way to define David's writing style actually; as a flow of easily distracted consciousness without the normal constraints of point, punchline, or punctuation.

It was raining the day we met for lunch. I arrived at the restaurant early and sat outside under a covered patio to watch the rain hitting the river. I was on my second wine when David arrived, twenty minutes late, and his first words to me were, "Fuck the traffic on King William Road, I could have walked here quicker but my hair would have got wet. Are we allowed to smoke out here?"

I've met a large amount of writers throughout my career - playwrights, journalists, poets, novelists. They all have something very 'writerish' about them and like to discuss past projects they've worked on, the current project they're working on, and the people they've worked on projects with. It's a legacy of focus and due to being locked away alone for long lengths of time. Writers don't get out much; devotion to their latest manuscript sacrifices family, friendships, and sunshine. With practically no social life, writers who find themselves thrown into a social situation will inevitably fall back on the subject of their current project. Good writers that is. Writers with focus. Writers who care and take their craft seriously.

David and I talked about chickens, dark tunnels, and tight socks. At one point we argued about which type of wood smells best. He told me his grandfather had been eaten by ants and asked how long I can hold my breath for.

Our conversation was much like reading one of David's books; refreshingly honest and unassuming one moment, oblivious to standard practices and social norms the next. Stating somebody's gingham shirt makes them look like a 'Canadian maple syrup farmer' is neither a compliment nor an insult to David, simply an observation. How the recipient interprets that observation isn't David's concern, as he's moved on to discussing hats for dogs and inflatable cars.

I rescheduled my meetings that afternoon and was late to work the next day; cheap saké administers its own unique form of punishment. I've heard there's a video floating about of David and me butchering Sinatra's *My Way* in a Japanese restaurant overlooking the River Torrens, but I haven't seen it so can't confirm or deny its existence. David slept on my couch that night. He wasn't there the next morning but he left a note that said, "I had a terrible time. Fuck you."

Which perhaps sums up David, and his style of writing, perfectly. *I Had a Terrible Time, Fuck You* should have been the title of this book.

Or at least the review on the cover.

Burning Bridges

While I was putting this book together, my offspring Seb asked what the title was going to be. When I told him the working title was *Burning Bridges to Light the Way,* he asked if it was a self-help book.

"It just sounds kind of... crystally."

"Crystally?"

"Like crystal healing. Or something to do with spirituality. It's the *Light the Way* bit I think. If you changed that part of the title it wouldn't sound so crystally."

"Change it to what?"

"I don't know, none of it really makes any sense. Why would anyone burn a bridge?"

"It's an old adage meaning once you have crossed a bridge, don't burn it because you never know when you might need to cross back."

"You could swim."

"Sure, that's not really the point though."

"Or build a raft and paddle across."

"If you were intending to go back, you shouldn't have burnt the bridge behind you. That's the point."

"What if you burnt the bridge and then realised you'd forgotten something? Like your mobile phone or car keys.

You'd feel pretty stupid then."

"Yes, probably. That's why the original adage is '*Don't* burn your bridges behind you'. The title about burning them to light the way is a play on that."

"It wouldn't provide much light for the trip ahead."

"Sorry?"

"The light would be behind you. You'd be much better off taking a flashlight."

"Right, I'll change the title to *Don't Burn Bridges, Just Take a Flashlight With You.* That's a lot better."

"And snacks."

Every year or so, when I release a new book, friends and associates state, "There'd better not be anything about me in your new book. If there is, and it's derogatory, I'll sue you."

Which is an empty threat because nobody I know has enough money to hire a lawyer. Most are one paycheck away from living in their car. Years ago, a coworker named Simon Edhouse threatened to sue me after I posted an email exchange between him and I on my website. It was a silly email, in which Simon asked me to design a logo and put together a few pie charts for free and I wasn't very helpful, but it went viral to the point where Craig Ferguson and Conan O'Brien mentioned it on their late night talk shows. I received several angry emails from 'Simon's lawyer' demanding I remove the exchange from my website, but they all contained several spelling errors and dozens of superfluous hyphens so I knew Simon had written them.

Once, he called me from a silent number and put on a Scottish accent and told me I had 48 hours to remove the post 'or else'.

"Or else what, Simon?"
"This isn't Simon. It's one of Simon's friends."
"Please. You don't have any friends."
"Yes I do, arsehole."

My coworker Ben, who suffers from Progeria, told me last week that if I write that he has Progeria once more, he's going to start his own website and post shit about me. When I asked, "What kind of shit?" he replied, "Stuff about you sucking your own dick!" so I guess it's going to be some kind of fan-erotica. Someone saying you have Progeria is hardly grounds for angry retaliation - it's not as if I wrote about the time I caught him masturbating to an episode of *Lazy Town*.

Melissa, our Chief Executive First Impression Officer, told me that if I ever use her last name, which is Peters, in an article, she will stab me in the throat with the yellow box cutter in her desk drawer. I've used her full name thirty-six times in previous books so if I'm discovered dead in my office with thirty-seven neck wounds, it will be because she finally got around to reading them. Jodie, our senior designer, has read a couple of my books and in one of them I wrote that during a three-hour drive to see a client, she ate four full size Snickers and a loaf of sliced bread. She was pretty cross about this because it wasn't a loaf of sliced bread, it was a baguette. The term 'fat-shaming' was used, and we had to have a meeting with Jennifer from HR, but, because I hadn't used Jodie's last name, which is Chapman, there wasn't anything that I could be reprimanded for. I said that I was talking about another fat girl named Jodie. A fat girl named Jodie Chairlamp. This was met with blank stares from Jodie and Jennifer, so for some reason I gave Jodie Chairlamp a backstory which included working at IKEA and owning two Labrador Retrievers.

My first book, *The Internet is a Playground*, contained several stories about a guy named Thomas deMasi - the Creative Director of a small branding company I'd worked for in Adelaide - and, when the book made the *New York Times Bestseller List*, he was interviewed by a reporter for the *Sydney Morning Herald* for an article titled, *Funnyman Of the Internet Just a Bully, Say Former Colleagues*. It was a fairly entertaining article in which a few former colleagues had a bitch session about articles I'd written about them, and Thomas was quoted as saying, "Humour born of someone else's humiliation is just easy humour."

Which isn't a great quote and doesn't make a lot of sense, but words were never Thomas' strong point. Once, during a client meeting with a frozen yoghurt company, he said the word yoghurt so many times it lost meaning and he starting saying yogamat. I get that some of the stuff I've written could be considered humiliating, but perhaps don't provide the content.

If you choose to tell everyone, "I have cancer and have two years to live," then it's discovered you made the whole thing up for attention, you can't just declare, "Humour born of someone else's humiliation is just easy humour!" when someone writes about you pretending to have cancer. Don't be a dickhead in the first place. After the SMH article came out, Thomas emailed me a link to it with the single sentence:

"Maybe this'll teach you not to burn bridges."

It was a fairly shitty bridge. One that I had no intention of crossing back over. It was like a rickety rope bridge that someone without an engineering degree cobbled together from rotten old wood pallets. The kind where one of the planks breaks as you're crossing and you almost fall to your death but your satchel gets caught and you use it to pull yourself back up. And there's some Arab looking guys hacking at the ropes with scimitars. Or maybe angry monkeys.

When you are angered by someone's words you consider humiliating, stating that they have burnt a bridge is simply hubris. Nobody likes to think their bridge is the angry monkey type of bridge even though most of them are.

"Behold my bridge. It is important and expansive. I should charge a toll to cross it."
"That's not a bridge, it's just a weathered rope swing with a stick tied to the end. It only gets you a third of the way across

and you have to let go at the right time and hope a leg doesn't get tangled which would mean being dragged back to the bank upside down."

"It's totally worth the effort."

"Is it though?"

"I have cancer."

Decent bridges don't burn easily. It's the rickety ones that go up like tinder. You'd need some kind of explosive device for a stone or metal bridge and this would take a bit of planning and maybe some knowledge about structural integrity weak spots. You'd also have to care a lot to go to the trouble and I honestly can't recall one single instance in my life where I've cared enough to *intentionally* burn any bridge by writing 'humiliating' things about anybody. There's a line I won't cross. It's a blurry line that I'll sometimes lean over to grab stuff, but I generally know which stuff is off limits.

I mean, it's not as if I've ever mentioned the time Thomas tore open his scrotum by putting his penis in a Shop-Vac hose and switching it on. Medical emergencies aren't funny and it must have been quite frightening. He needed stitches and had to wear a plastic cup, like a small version of the cone dogs have to wear around their neck, for two weeks. Not to stop him licking his scrotum, just to keep it clear of clothing.

I only learned about the Shop-Vac incident after Thomas and his flatmate, a guy named Dale who'd driven Thomas to the hospital that night, had a falling out over laundry detergent and Dale told everyone. It was definitely a betrayal of trust and either a statement of how much Dale cared about using the recommended dose of laundry detergent as shown on the label, or how little he cared about Bridge Thomas. When Thomas found out, he piled all of Dale's belongings on the curb and had the door locks changed. Homeless people took most of Dale's clothes, and his mattress, and Dale retaliated by group-emailing a video of Thomas he'd found on a flash drive in the kitchen junk drawer after breaking a window and climbing through to get his Xbox games and blender attachments.

The video featured a hairy bottom and a fairly impressive dildo, with a falsetto voice declaring, "Oh, Mister Jacobs, you're so big!"

Thomas denied it was him in the video - it was low resolution and shot from behind - but the likelihood of someone else having the exact same bedroom furniture, linen, and Rothko print above their bed, seems rather slim. Not that I have any problem with anyone putting things in their bottom. Go for it, the bigger the better. Impressive girth accommodation shows dedication, determination, and goal orientation, and, as such, should be included on resumes.

"Thank you for coming in today, Mister Smith. Your resume really stood out. It states here that you're able to dilate your sphincter to four inches?"

"Yes, that's correct."

"Very impressive. It must have taken a lot of commitment and many years to work your way up to that number. Do you have any way of verifying your credentials?"

"Pass me your coffee mug."

I have no idea who Mister Jacobs is...

From: David Thorne
Date: Thursday 3 October 2019 10.04am
To: Thomas deMasi
Subject: Mr Jacobs

Hello Thomas,

I see you are still active on social media so congratulations on beating cancer. Hope you are doing well. I'm currently writing the introduction to my new book and I was hoping you could help me clear up something.

In the video distributed during the Dale wars, the one of you showing dedication, determination, and goal orientation, who were you referring to when you declared, "Oh, Mister Jacobs, you're so big!"?

Regards, David

From: Thomas deMasi
Date: Thursday 3 October 2019 12.17pm
To: David Thorne
Subject: Re: Mr Jacobs

I've already told you that it wasn't me in that video and if you write that it was I'll fucking sue you for libel. I'm 100% serious. I'll get a copy of the book and check and if there's even one mention of my name in it, you'll be hearing from my lawyer.

....

I still have no idea who Mister Jacobs is. One of our clients was Jacob's Luncheon Meats though, so maybe Thomas just has a thing for Bung Fritz.

Regardless, Dale certainly burnt that bridge.

It's likely, along with Thomas, a few former and current associates will pick up this book to check if their names are mentioned. They'll mutter things like, "That fucking asshole better fucking not have mentioned the time I put three golf balls in my anus!" as they search through pages with narrowed eyes and even narrower lips. Occasionally their little snake tongue will flicker out and dart around as if also searching. As such, not wishing anybody to feel left out, here are twenty names to get the ball rolling:

1. Wayne Redding, of Modbury, Adelaide, put three golf balls in his anus. We were both thirteen at the time and he tried to convince me to also stick golf balls in my anus by showing me how easy it was to get them up if you rubbed margarine on them first. He was rather adamant that I try it and kept saying things like, "Just try it with one. Go on, this one is a clean one. It really doesn't hurt." When I refused to participate, Wayne attempted to choke me and I had to hit him with a Lego Millennium Falcon to get away. The next day at school, he told me he was only joking and hadn't really put the golf balls in his anus, it was a magic trick.

2. Shannon Walkley once shit herself at work. The smell permeated upstairs and when I went downstairs to find out where it was emanating from, I saw Shannon driving off with her chair in the back of her car. The next day, she explained that the chair had broken and she'd taken it to a 'chair repair place' to get it fixed. Unfortunately, there was nothing they could do and they had to throw the chair out because the 'main bit' was broken.

3. Nigel Matthews once catfished his sister Tanya on a dating site by creating a fake profile of a helicopter pilot named Jake. Tanya sent him several nude photos, including one of a Sharpie inserted in her anus, and Nigel used the photos to blackmail her into buying him a kayak.

4. Ross Amorelli shaves his back with a Bic disposable razor duct-taped to a stick. He has to shave his entire torso once a week or else his shirts won't fit.

5. Lucius Thaller once took a photo of his poo in the office bathroom and emailed the photo to his mother stating, "My poo is very yellow." His mother replied with, "Have you been eating a lot of bread? Your tummy might be reacting to the gluten."

6. In fifth grade, Tracy Williams urinated into a Styrofoam cup and Toby Dawson, the wheelchair kid, drank it for eighty cents and two Alf Pogs.

7. Geoff Leavesly, who works for Amcor as a sales representative, has a photo of his wife and son on his desk. Geoff isn't married and he has no children. The photo is from *iStock*. Someone told him Amcor prefers to employ married men so he changed his resume to include a wife and son, named Jackie and Matt, and purchased a wedding ring and a coffee mug that says *#1 Dad* from Amazon.

8. Matthew Buchanan stole the colour scanner from the computer room at UniSA in 1994. I saw him put it in his red Ford hatchback. A hundred dollar reward was offered for information about the theft so I made Matthew give me a hundred dollars and his parking pass not to tell. It's not as if we were friends, I saw him throw rocks at a goose once.

9. Simon Edhouse once backed up his failing hard drive to the work server and it took five hours because two folders, titled *NN01* and *NN02*, contained several thousand photos and videos of Japanese schoolgirls. There were no nudes; all were wearing swimsuits or school uniforms. Simon denied any knowledge about the folders but when I stated I was going to delete them to make room on the server, he became angry and shouted, "They're not mine so why would I care? Go ahead, delete them if you want. I really don't care. Why would I give a fuck? God I hate working with you people."

10. Andrew Snell has no left nipple. Apparently it's a medical condition called Athelia and there's a large market for rubber stick-on nipples. He has packs of five at home and keeps a couple in the glove box of his car. They're not cheap either, I stuck one to my cheek once and he made me give him thirty-five dollars.

11. Ray Paley, also of Modbury, Adelaide, sold his younger sister Cheryl's underpants from his locker at school. He started each sales pitch by giving them a sniff and saying, "These ones are good."

12. Jason Whitman wanked off his dog while we were watching *Simba the White Lion* in his living room. We were both nine and I didn't believe him when he said his dog's 'stiffy' got to the size of a shampoo bottle. He also ate a sandwich afterwards without washing his hands.

13. Tony Watson once sold two hundred raffle tickets for a charity that provides mowing and gardening services for the elderly. He bought himself a lawnmower and weed-whacker with the money, and his wife Linda won the raffle prize; a Weber three-burner barbecue. He did, however, offer a 15% senior-citizen discount with his new mowing and gardening service.

14. Sebastian Thorne hasn't washed his bed sheets in three months. His room smells like salt & vinegar chips.

15. Roger Hurst owns a life-sized rubber Realdoll® named Stephanie 2.0 that he paid over five grand for. His flatmate Nathan showed it to me while Roger was at work one day. The doll was very realistic and Nathan told me that whenever Roger went out, he had sex with it. Once, when Roger returned home unexpectedly, Nathan threw Stephanie 2.0 back in the wardrobe without cleaning up after himself. She was clean the next day though.

16. When I was eight, Steven Grovener tried to convince me to smell his mother's dildo. When I declined, he chased me, held me down, and stuck it in my mouth. I kept my teeth clenched but it went in my cheek. #MeToo

17. Oliver Mair's mother showed him how to wash his penis in a kitchen sink after a large amount of dick-cheese was discovered in his underpants. He was seventeen.

18. Lisa Evens sucked off a catering staff member behind a van at last year's SVBA Christmas party while her husband Dan was inside arguing the benefits of shower curtains over glass sliding doors with a guy dressed as an elf. I felt bad for Dan until I learned he hosts a bible reading group on Thursday nights at his house.

19. Ben Townsend has a thing for Stephanie from the children's television show *Lazy Town*. It's not a very big thing but it makes a big mess. Also, he has Progeria.

Above Ground Pools

20. When I was twelve, my best friend Michael Wilson told me an old guy wearing a hat gave him fifty dollars to suck his penis in the tennis court toilets at the end of our street. Fifty dollars was a lot of money to a twelve-year-old back then and I was far more jealous than shocked. I'd ridden my bike around the tennis courts hundreds of times over the years and was only ever offered a slice of pineapple by Mrs Dawson who lived across the road from the courts.

I'd once spent an afternoon at Mrs Dawson's house, playing with her son Jason, because my mother made me. Jason had muscular dystrophy and we spent four hours doing a jigsaw puzzle of London's Big Ben so I never went back. I'm pretty sure Mrs Dawson only chased me down with the pineapple to tell me Jason missed me and point out the fact that he was waving through the window. She made me promise I'd visit again but I heard Jason died so that was lucky.

I wrote 'London's' Big Ben above so you wouldn't get it confused with the 1960s television series, *Big Ben*, about a young boy's friendship with a bear. After writing the sentence before this one, I checked Wikipedia to see if *Big Ben* was broadcast in the 60s or 70s, and discovered it wasn't called *Big Ben* at all, it was called *Gentle Ben*, so I may have Alzheimer's. For those who haven't seen *Gentle Ben*, it was basically *Flipper* with a bear. All I remember of the series is that the boy's father rode through swampy marshes on one of those boats with a giant propeller on the back, and the bear always saved the day by tugging a rope. It wouldn't matter what the issue was, a bank robbery or bomb diffusion, the bear, which may have been named Ben but I'm not sure of anything anymore, tugged a rope. The boy would then make a rope related pun such as, "Guess they got roped into that one," and the father would laugh and tussle the boy's hair. Apart from coming up with a different rope related pun each week, working on the script must have been a pretty cushy job.

"Right, episode 82, there's a cattle stampede and the bear tugs a rope and saves the day."
"But it doesn't make any sense. Why are cattle stampeding in a marsh and how would tugging a rope stop them?"
"You're overthinking it, Greg, just work on the rope pun."
"Fine. How about, 'well he sure roped them in'?"
"Didn't we use that in the episode where the bear saved the school bus from going over a cliff by tugging on a rope?"
"No, that was, 'Ropey ropey rope rope'."
"Ah yes, not one of your best."

Apparently Michael didn't even have to suck the old guy's penis for the fifty dollars, he just stood there while the old guy sucked his.

"Who was he?"

"I don't know, just some old guy wearing a hat."

"And you just stood there?"

"No, I held his hat for him. And smoked a cigarette."

"Why were you smoking a cigarette?"

"The old guy gave it to me. He gave me the whole packet because there was only a few left. Do you want one?"

"No."

"Oh go on, it's cool. You know what we should do? Light a cigarette each and ride our bikes past Emma Jenkins' house while smoking them."

"Why?"

"So she'll know we're cool."

"Alright. What are you going to buy with the money?"

"More cigarettes."

I'd had a crush on Emma Jenkins since third grade but despite giving her a rare *Mork & Mindy* trading card and pretending to like *Alf* as much as she did, Emma hadn't shown any reciprocation. I changed into my basketball uniform before we left so Emma would know I was cool *and* sporty. Michael tucked the pack of cigarettes under his t-shirt sleeve, which was the fashion. We didn't have a second pack and I didn't have sleeves, so I tucked a box of Jell-O crystals into my sock to create a similar effect. We rode up and down Emma's street thirty or so times and while we couldn't be sure she saw us, as her house had those mirror windows you can see out of but not in, I'd like to think she did and said to herself, "I wish David was my boyfriend."

There's no way she would have wanted Michael to be her boyfriend because he had one leg shorter than the other and all of his left sneakers had a double sole. I know you can buy shoes that are made like that but Michael's family was poor so his dad just cut off the soles of old sneakers and glued them on. Michael also had bad asthma but looking cool outweighs the benefits of breathing, and he was on a pack a day within a few weeks.

The fifty dollars eventually ran out but Michael's mother was on a heavy regimen of painkillers after surgery to remove a brain tumor and never noticed money go missing from her purse. I'd been to Michael's house hundreds of times, slept over many nights, but his mother started introducing herself and asking if I went to the same school as Michael and if we were going swimming even if it was raining. They had a pool but it was one of those above ground Intex ones that you buy from Target and it was in their front yard so even if it was warm I never went in because people drove past and stared. The one time I did, a bus broke down outside.

"Do you want to go for a swim?"
"No."
"Oh come on, it's hot."
"No, people drive past and stare. Why didn't your parents put the pool in your backyard?"
"There isn't room."
"They could have moved all the old washing machines."
"No, too many snakes."

Michael's backyard contained at least fifty washing machines. His father repaired washing machines for a living and I guess he kept the broken appliances for parts, but most were rusty and half hidden by tall weeds that grew between them. Many of the washing machines were stacked two or three high and, if you squinted your eyes, it looked a bit like a city skyline. There was an old couch towards the back of the yard and we ran a couple of panels of corrugated tin roofing across two stacks of washing machines to make a shelter over it. It was a good place to hang out and smoke cigarettes until Michael was bitten by a snake and almost died.

I only smoked Michael's cigarettes at that point - maybe five or six a day. We smoked on our way to school, during recess and lunch break behind the gardener's shed, and on our way home. Sometimes we'd hang out at the local shopping mall to smoke and once Emma Jenkins walked past us with her parents and waved and her mother said, "I hope you're not friends with those boys. They smoke."

Emma smoked a cigarette with us behind the gardener's shed at school the next day. She didn't smoke a whole one but she took a couple of puffs of mine, which was pretty much the same as kissing because we shared germs. After she had the cigarette in her mouth, the filter tasted like cherry lip-gloss. I purchased my own pack of cigarettes that afternoon. I told the guy behind the counter at the local servo they were for my dad, not me, because I didn't think smoking was cool, and he said, "Like I give a fuck, homo."

I wasn't a homo though. I was cool. I lit a cigarette, tucked the pack under the sleeve of my *Ladyhawke* t-shirt, and rode the long way home to ensure as many people saw me as possible. The pack fell out a few times when I went over bumps (my mother only bought me clothes I'd grow into) so I used double-sided rug tape to secure it after that.

Kids don't need cigarettes to be cool nowadays of course, because they have vapes. There's nothing cooler than vaping. Especially those really big hits that hairy-necked fat guys named Cody do with toaster-sized vape-machines while they're walking down the street on their way to the comic store to argue about Captain Marvel's haircut with their friend Brandon who works there.

"And that's just four reasons why I should have won first prize, Holly. You can't just glue a peacock feather onto a Batman kite and... hey, look at that guy walking and vaping."
"Oh my god, he's so cool."
"I know. Every time he takes a big hit and walks through the smoke it's like that scene in *The Lion King* where Simba's dad sticks his head through a cloud."
"It really is. I wish we had friends like him."
"Me too. Our friends are terrible. We should start hanging out at local craft-beer breweries and cinemas that have Studio Ghibli marathons. Or bus stops."
"You'd have to leave the house more than once every six months."
"Oh, right. Never mind then."

I actually know a guy named Brandon who vapes. He only owns one shirt. I don't know him well but we do the tight lipped smile and nod when we see each other at events and he invited me to his wedding recently. I didn't go because it was a *Harry Potter* themed wedding and we had to bring our own wands. Brandon convinced me to try his vape once, it was a coffee-menthol-hibiscus blend that he'd mixed himself and called *Mistvana*. I wish I was making this up. I assume he has a special spot in his kitchen with dozens of little vape-oil bottles that he mixes and tries and nods and says to himself, "It's more of an art than a science."

"Rachel, try this blend..."
"Okay... hmm... it's very *coconutty*."
"Yes, I used coconut as the base, but can you identify the other flavours?"
"Mint and pomegranate?"
"No, despondency and self-disgust."

I also know a hairy-necked fat guy named Cody who vapes. He's like a human-sized slug but with more mucus and less ambition. I've never seen him walking while he vapes though, I've never seen him walk at all. He's always just sitting in a chair in a corner drinking somebody else's Pabst Blue Ribbon and sucking on his vape like the giant worm thing in *Alice In Wonderland*. I had a brief conversation with him at a party once but I honestly couldn't care less if Hawkeye plays a larger role in the 'graphic novels' than the Marvel Cinematic Universe so I left him there struggling to breathe and went outside to watch people playing 'hammer a nail in a log'.

"Join us, David. We're having a great time."

"No, that's okay, I don't know the rules."

"It's simple. Everyone has a nail and we take it in turns to hit someone else's nail with a hammer. Whoever's nail is last to be driven into the log is the winner."

"What do they win?"

"Another go."

"Why can't I just have normal friends?"

My friend Joseph recently broke up with his girlfriend Laura and, a week after the breakup, Laura had sex with Cody. Laura's not exactly a runway model herself, and I understand the psychological mechanics of rebound sex, but copulating with Cody would be like laying under a beached manatee while it grunts and thrashes for thirty seconds then rolls off, takes a vape hit, and explains the best sequence to watch the *Avenger's* movies in.

"...There are, of course, two common ways to build a Marvel movies timeline. The first is in release order, kicking off with 2008's *Iron Man*. The second is a chronological Marvel movie order, following the sequence of events. That means moving *Captain America: The First Avenger* to the pole position and shuffling Phase Three's movies in some interesting ways... are you crying?"

I don't know how I'd feel about this if I were Joseph. Was he relieved that Laura didn't select someone better than him, or concerned that it may have been a linear partner selection and ask himself, "Wait, am I a Cody?"

I asked Joseph these questions and he told me to fuck off so I guess he's still sensitive about the breakup. We all deal with grief in our way and I understand his feelings of loss; in certain cultures Laura might be considered quite a catch. In Uganda, for example, a particularly large woman can be worth five goats and a bolt of colourful fabric.

I was Facebook friends with Laura while she and Joseph were dating but I unfriended her last week. Not because of loyalty to Joseph, but because she posted, "I'm feeling sad about myself. Can all of my friends please say something they like about me?"

I mean, come on. How is this remotely acceptable? Post a photo of your cat or a meme and let the number of likes determine your self-worth like a normal person. I commented that particularly large women can be worth five goats and a bolt of colourful fabric in Uganda and hit the unfriend button.

Update: Apparently Laura and Cody are now seeing each other as Laura just posted, "Yay! Cody is taking me to Popeye's for lunch today."

I didn't see Laura's post, because we're not friends, but Holly sent me a screenshot to keep me in the loop. I've been to Popeye's and it's not all that. Laura's post received twelve likes and a "You go girl, so happy for you!" though, so she's probably feeling pretty damn good about herself right now. She might even put on pants and go inside instead of ordering at the drive-thru and eating in the parking lot. It's finding joy in small things that makes life worth living I guess - like the smell of freshly cut grass, or the sound of rain on a metal roof as you drift off to sleep, or a 'buy one, get one free' Popeye's voucher.

Update 2: Cody cancelled but he promised to take Laura to a Six Flags for her birthday.

Update 3: Cody bailed on the Six Flags promise. His car broke down and he had to spend the Six Flags funds on a replacement water pump. He bought Laura a fish for her birthday though. And a small plastic tank with neon green pebbles. Laura named the fish Goldy but Cody renamed it Excelsior.

Update 4: Laura and Cody had a massive falling out and are no longer seeing each other. According to Facebook intel, Cody used Laura's credit card to order a Nvidia GeForce RTX 2080 Ti and a subscription to Pornhub Premium. I'm less shocked by Cody's actions than the fact Laura owns a credit card. I'm not aware of her ever having a job and, just last year when she was pretending to have Tourettes and

Parkinson's Disease, she started a GoFundMe campaign to buy herself a wheelchair. Granted it was quite an expensive wheelchair, as it had to have special suspension or something, but that just makes it sad *and* audacious. My friend JM gave her fifty dollars towards it - which I was rather perturbed about as he'd already given her money towards a portable oxygen generator a few months prior when she was pretending to have Black Lung Disease. My bet is that in a week's time, Laura will have sex with a garbage bag full of puss and it will be Cody's turn to wonder if it's an upgrade.

Michael and I had a massive falling out when we were thirteen. It wasn't a violent argument, so nobody ordered pizza, but hurtful things were said and there was a lot of name-calling. I don't recall exactly how the disagreement started but I think it involved skateboard wheels. Or maybe the bearings. Regardless, the difference of opinion escalated quickly and our friendship ended when Michael told me he'd kissed Emma Jenkins and touched her boob behind the gardener's shed at school - and I told him I was going to tell everyone he let an old guy suck his penis in the tennis court toilets.

I didn't tell everyone that Michael let an old guy suck his penis in the tennis court toilets. I did ask Emma about the kissing and boob thing though. I knew it was a lie even before I asked because Michael and I were almost telepathically aware of each other's whereabouts every second of every day.

For the previous four years, I'd cut through a park each morning to get to Michael's house and waited for him to come out so we could ride to school together. We'd ridden home the same way, regardless of whether I was going over his house after school or not. We sat together in all the same classes, paired up on science projects and in gym, and spent every recess and lunch break together. There were no unaccountable moments in which he could have popped off for a quick snog and grope.

Emma confronted Michael about his claim and there was a bit of scene. Her honour had been besmirched and the only recourse was to publicly denounce Michael's fabrication by listing every reason why she would never physically interact with someone like him; He was ugly and small and poor and had one leg shorter than the other and had an above ground pool in his front yard and had a *Knight Rider* backpack and couldn't get through a single game of handball without having an asthma attack and... he had no friends.

The exhaustive denunciation took place at the bike racks after last class, to a large audience, and I watched, pretending I wasn't, from thirty feet or so away. Usually Michael and I parked our bikes together and shared a lock, but I'd chosen the rusty racks at the end that morning to make the point that even our bikes weren't friends.

Emma wasn't alone. Five of her friends stood behind her like a breakdancing crew, shouting both encouragement and insults. Michael denied saying he had touched Emma's boob but Emma and her B-girls weren't buying it. At one point it became physical and Michael's *Knight Rider* backpack was thrown onto the road and run over by a station wagon. His bike was also kicked over and, when he bent to pick it up, a large girl named Morgan whacked him across the back of his neck with a plastic ruler.

It's not much of a weapon but, in the right hands, a plastic ruler can deliver a pretty solid slap. The first and only time I ever wore shorts to school, Peter Jackson (not the director) slapped my thigh with a plastic ruler and it caused a huge welt that hurt all day. Years later, after we became friends, I reminded him of this and he said I could slap him with a plastic ruler to make it even. I didn't but I wanted to. Another popular weapon at our school, for a few weeks at least, was the hacky sack – a tennis ball-sized bag filled with beans that people with nothing better to do kick to each other. Nobody at school cared about hacky sacks until Sarah Hutchkins put one in a sock, swung it around her head, and belted Miranda Reynolds in the back of the head during gym. Everyone owned a hacky sack sock after that. The teachers thought it was some kind of new game until faction gangs formed and the red socks attacked the blue socks during assembly one afternoon. Advanced hacky sack sock technology was incorporated into the battle (two hacky sacks per sock) and four kids had to go to the school nurse - one to hospital. Hacky sack socks were banned after that and were replaced within a week by drink bottles filled with piss.

A week later, everyone had Super Soakers filled with piss. It meant recess and lunch were spent in long lines at water fountains and bathrooms, but a few entrepreneurial fifth graders sold full bottles for fifty-cents if you were low on ammunition.

Michael sprung upright with his hand to his neck. His face contorted and moisture welled in his eyes… a single tear escaped the surface tension and rolled down his cheek. It was a single tear too many and instantly placed his social standing just below Jasmine McKenzie who had wet her pants during a school excursion to a box factory two years earlier, and only slightly above Pinkshirt Fitzgerald* who called the teacher 'mum' at least once a week. For the next several months, whenever anyone recounted the event, they ended the story with, "And then Michael cried."

It was completely my fault. There was no way of knowing the whole thing would culminate in tears, but I knew, when I asked Emma about the kissing and boob touching, I was taking the argument about skateboard wheels - or maybe the bearings - to the next level. I wanted to win the argument, to be able to say, "Ha, I asked Emma about it and she said you were lying," but I also wanted Emma to be angry at him.

---

* *Pinkshirt's real name was Brian. He only wore a pink shirt to school once - after his mother washed his school uniform with his red hacky sack sock by accident - but the name stuck for two years until he developed bad acne and his name was changed to Driptray.*

As I watched Emma and her posse tear Michael apart like wolves on a limpy lamb, it didn't feel like I'd won. I wished I'd yelled, "Stop, Michael didn't really say he touched your boob, I was just making it up, hahaha, you fell for it." I wished I hadn't said anything to Emma in the first place. I wished that when Morgan threw Michael's *Knight Rider* backpack onto the road, I'd picked it up and returned it to him... and then performed a jumping triple roundhouse kick to Morgan's head. I wished, moments after the roundhouse kick, while everyone was exclaiming, "Oh my God, did you see what David did? He's like a Kung Fu Master!" a shimmering portal opened up a few feet above the ground and a robot stepped out and told me that I had to return to the future because I'd chosen to reveal my powers to protect a friend. A lot of my schoolyard fantasies involved portals for some reason.

Also, Holly made frittata for dinner tonight and I found a staple in my slice. This doesn't have anything to do with the story, I just wanted it on record in case it wasn't an accident. I've made a secret mark, like a swirly Freemason symbol, on the top corner of this page so you can find this paragraph again easily should I mysteriously pass away. Maybe let the authorities know to use a magnet during the autopsy.

I rode to school a different way the next morning, a bad way with lots of hills. I needn't have bothered, as Michael wasn't at school. Several kids came up to me throughout the day to tell me their unique version of the *And then Michael cried* story. One of the versions had Michael wetting his pants and crying for his mommy. Another had him wetting his pants, crying for his mommy, and being run over by a station wagon. I told them it wasn't true, that Michael had simply teared up a little from the pain of a cowardly plastic ruler attack while bent over, but they all knew someone who knew someone who had been there and witnessed it with their own eyes. I sat by myself in class, ate my lunch in the library with Toby the wheelchair kid, and rode home.

I've never had a large network of friends. I've told myself over the years that it's better to invest my time and energy in one or two good friends, rather than collect the whole set, but the truth is, I'm a bit of a selfish dick and far too lazy to put in the effort. I have no desire to go see a cover band of a band I've never heard of in the basement of an Ethiopian restaurant, or help anyone move furniture, or even look after somebody's cat while they're away on vacation. Just put it down and get a new cat when you get back. People give them away free. If I were someone else, I wouldn't be friends with me. What would I get out of it? A free book in December and the occasional sarcastic comment on Facebook? Fuck that.

I should have swum in Michael's stupid above ground pool in his front yard and played *Missile Command* on his Atari even though the game was old and nobody played Atari anymore. I should have told Dominic Murray his girlfriend Cheryl was cheating on him instead of accepting a remix of

Duran Duran's *The Reflex* on cassingle as a bribe from her to keep quiet about it. I should have stayed and helped JM pack his gear the last time we went camping instead of leaving him to get bogged in mud and needing to ask a guy with a tractor to drag his vehicle out. I should have asked Joseph if he was okay after he broke up with Laura instead of creating an online dating profile for him that stated he was 'a Mary Poppins carpetbag of surprises' and owned the world's largest rubber band collection. I should have answered my phone the night Peter Jackson (not the director) hung himself in his kitchen instead of nuking his call because I was in the bath.

In my defense, I only have a bath every two or three years. The decision to have one usually follows the random thought, "Ooh, I haven't taken a bath in years, that might be nice," but after filling the tub for an hour and sitting in it bored for five minutes, I remember why I don't take baths. It's like sitting in a really small pool. You're in water but there's nothing to do. You can't do laps or lay on a floatie, you just sit there like an idiot staring at your knees wishing you had a cigarette.

Holly likes having baths as she finds them relaxing. Her baths aren't relaxing for me though, as I'm somehow the one responsible for pre-bath preparation. This includes scrubbing the bath, drawing the bath, adding bubble bath and agitating the water, and lighting candles. I did it once for her because I was feeling guilty about something, and now it's become expected. Like backrubs. There's nothing worse than getting into bed, making yourself all comfy, and hearing, "Will you rub my back?" I usually pretend my arms are too sore from all the bathtub scrubbing and water agitation. Then, after Holly gets in the bath, the work really begins.

"You couldn't have made yourself a cup of tea before you got in the bath?"
"I didn't want a cup a tea then. I want one now."
"Fine. Any particular tea or just a Lipton jiggler bag?"
"Chamomile please. With a small drizzle of honey and a sprig of mint."
"Really?"
"Yes please."
"Right. Anything else? Would you like me to bake you some scones?"
"No thank you, just the cup of tea. And my iPad charger, earphones, my neck pillow, and a towel. Do we have any bath bombs?"
"No."
"Costco has them..."

I'm not a fan of Costco. For those unfamiliar with the store, it's like a sadder version of Wal-Mart for fat people. Costco charges a yearly $150 membership fee to get in but fat people are happy to pay this as they get a card with their photo on it. Apart from places like Weight Watchers and Planet Fitness, not a lot of clubs welcome fat people. Fat people see Costco as their Elks Lodge or church, but with packs of eighty toilet rolls for $39.95. Fat people go through a lot of toilet paper. That's not being sizeist, it's a fact, and has less to do with the size of their huge poos than the surface area to wipe afterwards. I shared an apartment with a fat guy named Glen Williams many years ago and he went through two rolls a day. He used rolls of paper towels instead of toilet paper, as paper towels are heavier duty and can be folded more times than toilet paper, but this only reinforces my point. Glen also kept a spray bottle of water by the toilet. And a plunger. We eventually had a falling out over cleaning duties and I moved out. Years later, after Glen was told he wouldn't live past his thirties due to his weight, he applied for the Australian version of *The Biggest Loser* and appeared on season two in 2007. He dropped nearly a hundred pounds during the show, but was sent home in episode five after a cache of Mars Bars was discovered under his mattress. He kept up the exercise though, jogging every day, and was down to three hundred pounds when he was hit and killed by a Prius. You just can't hear them coming. I attended his funeral. I wasn't going to, as we hadn't seen each other in years, but I'm glad I did. Bob Harper and Jillian Michaels (the American personal trainers from the show) were at the service and Jillian introduced me to her personal assistant, Holly. My hair was looking good that day so I asked Holly out, and three years later we were married. Also, Jillian Michaels is a bit of a bitch in real life. I can't elaborate, as a non-disclosure agreement was signed, but let's just say Jillian is a yeller and doesn't like people using her pool when she's not home.

Holly joined Costco last year; she's not fat but likes a bargain, and one of her fat friends spoke highly of the price of toothpaste there. I've no idea what a tube of toothpaste usually costs, but if you buy fifty tubes of toothpaste for twenty cents less than normal price, you save ten dollars and won't need to buy toothpaste for several years, which also saves time writing it on shopping lists. I've only been to Costco once with Holly and I'm never going back. For the price of entry, you'd think they could give you bags to put your thirty-pack of socks and sixty-pound bags of sugar in, but no, after you've carried in the groceries at home, you have to work out what to do with twenty empty weirdly shaped avocado and mouthwash boxes. Also, most of their stuff isn't even real brand name products, it's something called Kirkland. I'm sure you're pretty safe with Kirkland carrots, but Kirkland wine, mayonnaise, and ibuprofen? Also, where are people storing their 40-gallon drums of Kirkland ice cream?

"Ooh, we need paper towels. Grab them."

"Do we need that many, Holly?"

"You can't have too many paper towels and two hundred rolls for $199 means they're less than a dollar each. That's a bargain."

"I like Bounty."

"Kirkland is just as good."

"Is it though? You said that about their cheese and it tasted like paint. Besides, where are we going to store two hundred rolls of paper towels?"

"In the garage. We can park on the street. Ooh, that means there'll be room for that four-hundred-box pack of breadcrumbs in aisle seven and the fifty-pack of pillows in aisle ten. Grab the paper towels and we'll do another loop of the store."

"Fine, then can we look at the televisions?"

"We don't need a television."

The next day was a Saturday. It was warm and cloudless. Usually Michael and I spent Saturdays skateboarding on the tennis courts at the end of the street until someone would yell at us to get off because we we're leaving marks on the surface, or we'd ride our bikes to a pond we had discovered and smoke cigarettes.

Once when we rode our bikes to the pond, there were a group of teenagers already there. They threw our bikes in the pond and we had to wade in and drag them out. The pond wasn't very deep but the mud went down a long way and Michael lost his special left shoe with the double sole. His bike pedals were the metal spiky kind so he had a lot of trouble riding home. He also had to wear a rubber rainboot with thick socks to school for a few days until his dad made him a new shoe.

Another time when we rode to the pond, we heard voices so we hid our bikes in the brush and crept forward to look over an embankment. A teenage couple was kissing below us. The boy had his hand down the front of the girl's jeans and she was giggling and telling him to stop. Suddenly, the boy leapt up and rushed to the edge of the pond. He knelt down, reached out into the water, and lifted out a turtle.

"Check this out," he said, holding the turtle up to show the girl, "I caught a turtle."

"What are you going to do with it?" asked the girl.

"Smash its shell," the boy replied. He put the turtle on the ground, looked around until he found a decent sized rock, and raised it above his head.

A fist-sized rock hit the boy in the side of his head, throwing him sideways into the water. The girl screamed. I looked around, and up, at Michael. He was on his feet, a second rock ready, with a look of pure anger on his face. The boy sat up in the water, lifted his hand to his head unsteadily, and pulled it away covered in blood. Michael leapt over the embankment, grabbed the turtle, and yelled, "Run!" as he legged it past the boy and girl into the woods. It was pretty much the second bravest thing I've ever seen anyone do.*

Michael named the turtle Ace Frehley and kept him in his above ground swimming pool for a few days until his mother made him take it back to the pond. It was probably for the best as their pool was over-chlorinated and Ace Frehley just sat on a boogie board looking sad. Every time we went to

---

* *I flicked a snake off our patio furniture with a stick once.*

the pond after that and saw a turtle, Michael declared, "That's Ace Frehley, I can tell by the shell."

He said it about a flat rock once though so there's no way of knowing if he was ever right. One time however, he waved to a turtle sitting on a partly submerged tree branch and called out, "Hello, Ace Frehley," and, I kid you not, the turtle lifted its front foot for a few seconds as if waving back. Maybe it *was* Ace Frehley. Maybe turtles just lift their legs sometimes.

Instead of spending my Saturday morning skateboarding or riding to the pond, I whacked a tree with a stick in our backyard and went to Target with my parents to buy beanbags. We already owned four but needed two more for guests.

That afternoon, while I was lying on my bed staring at the ceiling, I came up with a plan. A genius plan that would fix everything; I'd light a cigarette and ride my bike past Michael's house. He'd see me and come out and ask, "What's up?"

"Nothing," I'd reply, "Just riding my bike around and smoking cigarettes... Oh yeah, sorry about asking Emma if you touched her boob, I didn't say anything about you letting an old guy suck your penis in the tennis court toilets for fifty dollars though."

"Cool," Michael would nod, "Thanks for not telling anybody about that."

Then, and this is the genius part, I'd accidently drop a sandwich bag containing chopped up pieces of ham out of my pocket. Michael would ask what the ham is for and I'd reply, "Oh, that? I was thinking about riding to the pond and feeding it to Ace Frehley. You can come with me if you want."

I practiced both my script and dropping the bag in the mirror a few times before I left. There was no ham in the fridge so I cut up some cheese instead.

Michael was in his pool with Pinkshirt Fitzgerald. They were splashing about and having a lot of fun. Michael's mother sat on the front step, laughing and clapping at their efforts to do handstands underwater. This wasn't according to plan so I stopped my bike on the sidewalk, a few feet from the pool, and did the universal gesture for 'what the fuck?'

"Is that one of your school friends, Michael?" his mother asked.
"No," replied Michael, "We're not friends. He wanked off his dog."
"Well let him know he dropped his bag of cheese."

It's outrageous that an accusation without any foundation can become a rumour. For the next three or four years, kids came up to me and asked if I really wanked off my dog. Kids I didn't even know, kids from different schools. I heard several different versions as well, one of them had me kissing my dog while I wanked him off and another had me wanking him off into a cup. Whenever the word dog was mentioned, in the schoolyard or by a teacher in class, everyone turned to look at me. It was very frustrating and probably how Richard Gere feels when anyone mentions gerbils. I have no idea why Michael decided on the whole wanking off a dog thing. A year or so before I had told him about another kid, named Jason Whitman, who had wanked off his dog to prove how big the dog's stiffy got, but I didn't participate in the dog wanking, I just said, "Eww, it looks like a maraca."

I told everybody that Michael had let an old guy suck his penis in the tennis club toilets for fifty dollars, and had held his hat, but this was met with the response, "You just made that up because he told everybody you wanked off your dog."

Michael and Pinkshirt Fitzgerald became best friends. They rode to and from school together every day and smoked cigarettes behind the gardener's shed. Every time Pinkshirt called the teacher 'mum' in class, I glanced at Michael, who sat several desks away, and he'd glance back at me then quickly look away. I pretended I didn't care that we weren't friends and started hanging out with a kid named Dustin - who everyone called Dustbin. Dustbin's house had an inground pool in the backyard and he became my new best friend for a few years until we had a falling out over a *Jeff Wayne's Musical Version of War of the Worlds* album - or maybe the booklet in it.

I saw Michael twenty-five years later. I was working for a small design agency called DeMasi Jones at the time. We'd completed a branding commission for Bridgestone Australia's B-Select retail stores and I was visiting one of the outlets during a refit to check the signage. I stepped outside to have a cigarette and saw Michael, up a ladder, painting a giant B. He didn't notice me but I knew the extra glued-on sneaker sole anywhere. I considered, for a moment, butting out my cigarette and going back inside before he recognized me, but our falling out had been many years before and I'm not one to hold a grudge.

"You missed a spot."

"What? Where? ...David?"

"Long time no see, Michael. Been sucked off by any old guys in tennis court toilets lately?"

"No. Wanked any dogs off lately?"

"That never happened."

"So you say. You got a spare cigarette?"

"No."

I thought about rewriting the above paragraph, maybe making something up about us hugging it out and starting a turtle sanctuary together, but fuck him. Five years after our falling out, while I was on a camping trip in a different state, a kid came up to me and asked if I'd really wanked off my dog.

Brave

From: David Thorne
Date: Thursday 17 October 2019 2.47pm
To: Michael Wilson
Subject: Turtle

Hello Michael,

I'm currently working on a project that reminded me of the time you leapt over an embankment and rescued Ace Frehley from having his shell crushed.

I just wanted you to know that it was the second bravest thing I have ever seen anyone do. I don't think I told you at the time and I should have.

Regards, David

....

From: Michael Wilson
Date: Friday 18 October 2019 11.01am
To: David Thorne
Subject: Re: Turtle

Okay. Thanks I guess. What was the first bravest?

From: David Thorne
Date: Friday 18 October 2019 11.16am
To: Michael Wilson
Subject: Re: Re: Turtle

I flicked a snake off our patio furniture with a stick.

David

....

From: Michael Wilson
Date: Friday 18 October 2019 11.28am
To: David Thorne
Subject: Re: Re: Re: Turtle

How is that braver? How big was the snake?

....

From: David Thorne
Date: Friday 18 October 2019 11.33am
To: Michael Wilson
Subject: Re: Re: Re: Re: Turtle

The size of the snake isn't important.

David

Office Fight

A fight broke out in the office a few minutes ago and is well underway. No punches have been thrown but Melissa and Jodie have declared, "Fuck it, gloves off; I'm all in. I am no longer bound by social norms or fearful of reprise and will hurt you as much as I can with words at the highest volume I can muster."

Apparently the fight started when Jodie described Melissa's nail polish colour as, "a bit 2015." I'm not sure how it escalated, as I was in the bathroom, but I heard yelling and exited in time to witness Melissa throw a 6" Subway sandwich at Jodie. The sandwich barely glanced Jodie's shoulder, but she reacted as if hit by a .50 caliber round, screamed, "That's assault you fucking bitch!" and knocked a framed photo (of Melissa and her boyfriend Scoutmaster Andrew sitting on a petrified log) off Melissa's desk. Melissa's response focused on Jodie's weight so it's definitely on...

...Right. Jodie's in tears and she attempted to push the photocopier over but only succeeded in breaking off the paper tray. It's the most exciting thing to happen here all week so I'm going to cover this live as the action unfolds...

Update: 10.48am

Jodie is sitting in her car talking on her phone. I don't know who she's talking to but I hope it's the police. In her absence, Melissa is explaining to us her side of the story. As encouragement, we're agreeing that she's in the right and affirming we've always liked her more than Jodie...

Update: 10.55am

Melissa just leaped over the line and chose the nuclear option by disclosing personal information Jodie told her in confidence. I'm not sure how all of us knowing Jodie has genital herpes helps Melissa's argument but her commitment to take the situation to 'raining fire' level is to be applauded...

Update: 11.01am

It's like an episode of Survivor where one contestant lists the reasons someone else should be voted off instead of them. The entire office is now also aware that Jodie tore her anus a few months ago and had to have stitches, owes petty cash $340 for a loan to make rent, and sucked off the rep from Smucker's Jam in his Ford Edge...

Update: 11.08am

Jodie just reentered the office and a heated exchange about who is the bigger bitch ensued. Apparently Melissa is the biggest bitch Jodie has ever met but Jodie is the biggest bitch in the world so that wins. Jodie retaliated with, "At least I don't buy my jeans from Old Navy!" and did a weird wiggle of the head with a smirk. I'm not sure how that's an insult as I own jeans from Old Navy and they're pretty comfy, but it seemed to outrage Melissa who screamed, "They're from H&M bitch!"...

Update: 11.15am

Melissa has "had enough of stupid fat bitches" and went to Subway to purchase a replacement sandwich. It's therefore Jodie's turn to seek affirmation from everyone in the office that she's in the right and explain why Melissa should be voted off the island...

Update: 11.19am

I asked Jodie if she really sucked off the rep from Smucker's Jam and she's sitting in her car again...

Update: 11.25am

Jennifer from HR is sitting in Jodie's car with her. She had to tap on the window for a few minutes before Jodie unlocked the passenger side and let her in. I'd give a toe to hear the conversation as Jodie is waving her arms about like she's summoning a water demon...

Update: 11.39am

How am I the bad guy? Jennifer just spoke to me about 'unnecessary escalation of sensitive situations' (which can't possibly be a real HR term) and Jodie gave me a death glare on her way to the kitchen. Rebecca, the office gossip, has gone to "check if Jodie is okay," which can be translated as, "I'm going to tell Jodie everything Melissa said so you might all want to put on safety goggles."...

Update: 11.52am

'OMG' isn't a term I throw about, as I'm not a 15yo girl on a bus, but OMG! Jodie just stormed up the stairs and declared, "Not that it's anyone's business but yes, like 47% of the population, I have herpes okay? Like none of you have ever had unprotected sex."

She neither confirmed nor denied sucking of the rep from Smucker's Jam, but she did inform us that Melissa had an abortion when she was 16 and cheated on Scoutmaster Andrew with an electrician named Greg...

Update: 11.56am

I checked Jodie's statistics and only 11.9% of the population have genital herpes. The 47% is people who have them on their face - which still seems like a lot. I'm not sure how correcting her error makes me an asshole but apparently "it just does"...

Update: 12.08pm

Jodie is sitting in her car again. According to Jennifer, asking a coworker how they tore their anus is borderline sexual harassment but I was only asking so I don't do it accidentally. Melissa returned and is eating her Subway sandwich at her desk. It would have been polite to ask if anyone else wanted anything from Subway. I considered going out to get an Egg McMuffin and loudly asking if anyone else wants anything from McDonald's to make a point, but I'm not leaving in case I miss anything so it's Mentos for lunch...

Update: 12.19pm

I'm glad I didn't leave. Mike, our creative director, just came back from a meeting and said to Melissa, "What's with the sour face? You should smile whenever someone walks in the front door." and Melissa replied, "Go fuck yourself, Mike. I quit."...

Update: 12.25pm

Jennifer, Mike and Melissa are having a meeting in the boardroom. Jodie came back in and I told her the meeting was regarding her unprovoked aggressive behaviour, so she's stormed in to set the record straight. I should probably be in that meeting as I was the only witness to the Subway sandwich assault...

Update: 12.44pm

I explained to Jennifer and Mike there was a bee in the office and that Melissa swiped at it with her Subway sandwich and lost her grip. Jodie accused me of taking sides so, for balance, I suggested that angry outbursts over small things can often disguise larger issues, such as feeling bad about cheating on Scoutmaster Andrew with an electrician named Greg.

I could probably be some kind of conflict resolution counselor if I ever decide to change careers. Jennifer asked me to leave...

Update: 12.58pm

They've been in the boardroom for over 30 minutes now and I'm getting bored. Really it should be a group discussion as we were all involved and I've thought of 4 more helpful things to say. One of them involves hand sanitizer.

I tried listening at the door but Ben is printing out an annual report and I can't hear anything over the noise. Gary, our account rep, opened the door to ask if anyone knew how to fix the photocopier and was yelled at, but apart from that there's nothing new to add...

Update: 1.10pm

They're still in there. I've thought of 5 helpful things to say now and I'm beginning to suspect Jennifer only asked me to leave because she was intimidated by my natural conflict resolution abilities. Number 5 is based on the Aesop's tale about the crow and fox but tweaked to be about two pigs fighting over a cob of corn...

Update: 1.28pm

The meeting is over and it's all a bit of an anti-climax I'm afraid. In an obvious effort not to be shown up, Jennifer brought her HR A-game and a ceasefire has been called.

Actually, ceasefire may not be the appropriate term - it's more like a school play about friendship; Melissa is back at her desk and Jodie just walked past her and asked, "I'm going to make a cup of tea, would you like one?" and Melissa replied, "No, but thank you for asking."

I'm quite disappointed as I was hoping to be the hero by defusing the situation with my story about corn. It's wasted now. I might still email it to them though...

....

From: David Thorne
Date: Wednesday 14 August 2019 1.34pm
To: Melissa, Jodie
Subject: Corn

It was a warm day and two pigs were enjoying the cool mud in their sty. One spotted a cob of corn and showed it to the other.

"Look what I have found," the pig exclaimed, "it's a delicious cob of corn."
"Yes," replied the second pig, "we should share it."
"Why?" asked the first pig, "I found it so it's mine."

"Well that's not very nice," the second pig lamented, "I thought we were friends."

"Yes, so did I," nodded the first pig, "until I found out you told everyone about my herpes."

Little did they realize they had bigger things to worry about as it was slaughter day at the farm and, really, a cob of corn wasn't worth destroying a friendship over. They're about a dollar for four at the supermarket.

I think there's something in that for all of us, Melissa and Jodie. Feel free to print it out and tape it to the wall over your desks if you'd like.

Regards, David

....

Update: 1.55pm

Gary fixed the photocopier with duct-tape and nobody likes my story about corn.

Gossip

It began in the small village of Harrisonburg, Virginia, but, like an airborne super-virus with no known cure, it spread rapidly. Within minutes it was in Chicago, hours later there were reports that it had spread to New York, Los Angeles, Mexico City, London, Sydney...

Jack O'Reilly had no contact with the outside world. He lived off the grid, in a small log cabin by a river, on a heavily forested property his great, great grandfather had hunted on. The nearest town was a ten-day trek away and it had been almost twenty years since he'd last had human contact. He had no need or desire for modern technologies; he made his own lamps from beaver fat and the forest provided wood for the stove and meat for his belly. There were large bass in the river and that morning, he'd risen at first light and made his way down a well-worn trail with his fishing rod. He sat on the edge of the bank and cast his line... A canoe came around the bend and a lone paddler waved frantically.

"Hello? Jack?" Lori yelled to him, "Seb spent all of his money on computer parts and is flying to America broke. I just thought you should know."

Business Cards

Joseph opened the box containing his new business cards excitedly. He'd ordered them from Vistaprint and waited a week for them to be delivered. They'd advertised a hundred cards for $9.99, but he'd opted for the matte finish, gold lettering, and a logo he'd designed, so they ended up costing a few hundred more. It was worth it though; the logo had come out nice. It featured two people, a black person and a white person, giving each other a high five while jumping over a rainbow. There was also a dove, a wand, and a chain with broken links.

He'd met a black girl on Tinder a few weeks before. She smoked cigarettes so they had a lot in common. On their first date he showed her the wooden spoons he'd hand carved and gave her one for free. The relationship meant a lot of changes of course. Not for him, for everyone else. Nobody was allowed to make racist jokes anymore, not even ones about bicycles, and they weren't allowed to sing along to rap songs.

Joseph held up one of the cards and nodded approvingly at his new title: *Civil Rights Activist.* He'd chosen the Jumanji typeface.

Looks Good, Let's Go

I read that Keith Flint, the lead singer of The Prodigy, committed suicide today. He took his dog for a walk, went for jog, and then hanged himself. There seems to be a lot of that going around at the moment. Not the dog walking or jogging bit, the hanging.

I've had three close friends take their own lives over the years. Peter Jackson (not the director) hanged himself after finding out his girlfriend slept with seven guys at a party (not at the same time, they took turns), Simon Dempsey gassed himself in his car because his girlfriend slept with a white-water rafting instructor while she was on holiday with her sister, and Craig Leavesly hanged himself accidently while having a wank. Craig also had a girlfriend who cheated on him but he didn't care because she was ugly and fat and he was only dating her because she worked at a pawn store called Cash Converters and could get him cheap PlayStation games.

I'm not sure what the attraction of choking yourself while you masturbate is but apparently it's a thing. I prefer to light a candle, put on some background music - maybe something by Michael Bubble - and masturbate inside a garbage bag with two holes cut out for my legs like a normal person.

I saw The Prodigy play live in the mid-nineties and still have the scar to prove it. They toured Australia and while I wasn't all that familiar with their music, my best friend at the time, Thomas Harrer, was a massive fan. Thomas had both of their CDs and called them the The Prodge! He had a thousand dollar stereo installed in his five-hundred dollar Datsun 180B primarily for the track *Their Law* and I probably heard it a thousand times.

"Yes, it's a decent track, but would you mind turning it down a notch? I'm getting bruised."
"That's not the volume, it's the subwoofer. It puts out ten thousand whogivesafucks and is twelve-feet wide. I had to have an extension built onto the back of the Datsun to house it. I'd turn it up so you can see what it's really capable of but the doors fall off."

I don't have a vivid memory of the concert, as it was the first time I ever tried ecstasy, but I remember it was loud and colourful and a girl wearing furry boots fell off a speaker and broke her arm. There were a lot of girls - and a few guys - wearing furry boots at the concert so it must have been a popular rave fashion at the time. I'd actually felt a bit self-conscious standing in the line to go in; while other concertgoers were dressed in colourful raver outfits and sporting dozens of glow-stick bracelets, I was wearing jeans, tennis shoes, and a t-shirt that I'd bought at the Adelaide Zoo with an otter on it.

"You didn't tell me it was a dress-up concert, Thomas. I would have worn something more fun otherwise."

"You don't own anything fun."

"Please. What about my t-shirt with the word Helvetica written in Times New Roman? That's fun."

"Not really."

"Yes it is. I bet if I'd worn it a lot of people here would have smiled and said, 'Ha. Clever.'"

"It's more of a graphic designer joke than a funny one."

"I've got one that says Times in Helvetica as well. I don't like that one as much though, the kerning's out."

"There's a booth selling tour t-shirts over there. Get one and change in the bathroom."

"I'm not paying twenty dollars for a Gildan t-shirt. They're itchy and shrink to half the size when you wash them. Besides, the line is too long."

"Don't worry about it then. A lot of people like otters. And going to the zoo. Children mostly."

There was a girl wearing furry boots in front of us in the tour t-shirt line. She was also wearing a matching furry jacket even though it was summer and she must have been uncomfortable, a pair of yellow glasses with no lenses that were about four times as large as normal ones, and she was sucking on a Chuppa Chup.

"You wanna buy some e?" the girl asked.

"No, thank you," I replied, "We're just in line for the t-shirts."

"We'll take four," said Thomas.

I've never really been much into drugs. I smoke marijuana from time to time (8am to 11pm) and I've tried practically everything else once, but the fear of making a spectacle of myself in public has always overridden the fun of being high. Perhaps I should just 'loosen up a bit', as has been suggested, and inject heroin into my eyeballs, but at this point in my life I'd rather spend the money on power tools and plants.

"Okay, well I'm off. Have a good weekend, David."
"You too. Anything exciting planned?"
"Yes, I'm attending a rave in a forest. The only way to get there is by ATV but Bassnectar is playing so it should be worth the two-hour ride. I'm going to take a lot of drugs and have sex with girls wearing furry boots. Yourself?"
"Going to plant a birch."
"Nice."
"Yes, I'm a big fan of the birch."

I met a heroin addict once. It's possible I've met others and didn't realize because they were 'high-functioning' addicts, but the one I met was one of the barely-functioning ones. Her name was Simone and she was in her early twenties but looked a lot older - like a blonde Iggy Pop. I was nineteen and had invited a handful of people over for a house-warming party after moving into a new apartment. Twenty or so people came and went that night, mostly friends of friends, many of which I'd never met. Simone was one of them and she had her four-year-old son with her.

The toddler sat quietly playing *Sonic the Hedgehog* on my Sega Mega Drive for most of the night, but was curled up on my sofa asleep when Simone left. There was no mention about looking after the child, or indication when she was coming back, she just left him. Like someone might leave a packet of cigarettes or sunglasses behind.

Around midnight, after everyone had left, I draped a blanket over the child and went to bed. In the morning, I made him toast and we played video games. His name was Jacob and he liked *Thomas the Tank Engine*. There was still no sign of his mother by mid-morning so I called around and one of the friends of a friend knew the street Simone lived on, but not the house number.

I stacked a couple of pillows on the passenger seat of my car, buckled Jacob in, and drove to the street he lived on. We agreed, during the drive, that hedgehogs aren't blue in real life. I'm not sure why that's memorable. He was very astute for a four-year-old and pointed out his house and his mother's car when we drove slowly down the street. I pulled into the driveway behind a rusty Honda Civic hatchback with a faded yellow 'Baby on board' sign suction-capped to the back window. There was a plastic playset in the front yard, with steps to a small slippery-dip and turnable blocks of tic-tac-toe. The colours were bleached by the sun and one of the tic-tac-toe blocks was missing. The slippery dip part had a large crack in it and was lying several feet away from the playset in long grass.

An upstairs window was open and I could hear music but there was no answer when I knocked on the door. Jacob reached up on tippy toes and turned the handle to let himself in. I followed him into the living room and shouted up the stairs. There was no reply.

"She's in the bath," Jacob told me, "She listens to music when she's having a bath and I have to stay downstairs and be good."

I stayed with him for about fifteen minutes - watched as he pottered about picking up trash and emptying ashtrays. There was a potted plant on top of an old Teac television set that may have once been a Ficus. Three Christmas tree decorations hung from the dead branches - two silver balls and a Sydney Opera House fridge magnet with string taped to it - even though it was nowhere near Christmas. The couch, salmon velour, had seen better days. Better decades really. The arms were torn and the underlying foam was dry and brittle. The style was like something you'd buy from Shewel's. There was no other furniture.

At one point Jacob disappeared into the kitchen and I heard running water so looked in. He'd pulled a chair over to the counter, climbed up on it, and was washing the dishes in the sink. When he was done, he took a cloth and crawled over the countertops, wiping them down. I asked if he was going to be okay and he nodded. I asked if he needed anything and he shook his head.

I dropped the Sega Mega Drive and my collection of games off at Jacob's house a few days later. I didn't really play it much. The upstairs window was open and I could hear music, but nobody answered when I knocked so I left it on the porch. I hope he got to play it a few times before Simone took it to Cash Converters.

"Taking drugs wasn't in the itinerary, Thomas."
"It was in mine."
"What kind are they?"
"What do you mean what kind?"
"Are they the kind where I say, 'Hmm, that was interesting', or the kind where I end up climbing through people's windows?"
"Why would you climb through people's windows?"
"To steal their televisions. So I have money for my next fix. That's what addicts do. They sell stolen televisions at Cash Converters."
"The first kind then."
"What will they do to me?"
"They'll make you feel good."
"That's a pretty broad statement. Nobody would buy drugs if they made you feel bad. They could drink spoiled milk for free. Will they cause me to make a spectacle of myself in public?"
"They might cause you to dance."
"I'm definitely not taking them then."
"Loosen up a bit. You'll have fun."
"I don't need drugs to have fun."

"Yes you do. You're the least naturally fun person I know."

"Why would you say that?"

"Because it's true."

"No it isn't, I'm barrels of fun."

"Name one thing you've done this year that's fun."

"I went to the zoo."

I can't dance. I've tried on several occasions and fully accept the fact that I look like a marionette walking up stairs while holding two lit candles. People have declared, "Of course you can dance, David, you're just being self-conscious, stop worrying about what anyone else thinks and simply move your body to the beat." But then if I do, they say, "Okay, perhaps you should stop. Are all of your other motor-skills intact? Can you drive a car with a manual gearbox?"

I wish I could dance. I'd dance all the time. I'd be that fun partner that drags Holly onto the dance floor and cuts loose in a fashion nobody would ever describe as pushing a wheelbarrow through mud or inflating an air mattress with a foot pump while playing Whac-A-Mole. People would say, "Gosh, David, you're an amazing dancer. Have you considered dancing professionally?" and I'd reply, "No, I only dance for the love of it. But thank you though."

I took one of the pills in a bathroom cubicle while I was changing shirts. The t-shirt booth had run out of my size by the time we got to the front of the line but I managed to squeeze into a small and stretched it as much as I could.

The square graphic on the front (the CD cover of *Music For the Jilted Generation*) became a wide rectangle and a sleeve seam tore, but my otter t-shirt slipped off the toilet seat and fell onto the floor into a puddle of urine, so I had no choice but to go with it.

"Looks good, let's go."

"It's a bit tight, Thomas. And short. I think they sold me a women's small."

"Just pull your pants up higher to cover your belly button."

"Like this?"

"Okay, maybe don't do that. Try pulling the shirt down a few inches."

"It's stretched as far as it will go. If I pull it down any harder the sleeve will come off. I knew it was a mistake buying a Gildan t-shirt."

"Maybe change back into your otter t-shirt then."

"I can't. It fell into a puddle of urine so I flushed it. Or at least tried to. It must have been a polyester blend because it trapped a big air bubble and wouldn't go down."

"Looks good, let's go."

"Looks good, let's go" is the same thing my partner Holly says whenever she's in a hurry to leave the house and I ask if I should change. It wouldn't matter if we were meeting the Queen and I was wearing just a sock.

"Almost ready, Holly. I just have to change my shirt."

"Why? Looks good, let's go."

"It has a spaghetti sauce stain on the front."

"You can hardly notice it. Looks good, let's go."

"There are chunks of tomato and strands of spaghetti."

"Looks good, let's go."

"I have some in my hair as well."

"Looks good, let's go."

I once left the house with my jacket inside out, two different shoes on, and a piece of chocolate stuck to the back of my jeans. Holly has heated seats in her car and the chocolate melted and I pushed a trolley around a supermarket for an hour looking like I had shit myself. An old lady eventually tapped me on the shoulder and pointed it out but we were in the checkout line by then.

"Excuse me."

"Yes, I'm fully aware the sign says 15 items or fewer."

"No, I just wanted to let you know your jacket is inside out. I can see the tag."

"Oh my god, thank you for pointing that out. How embarrassing. I blame my wife entirely for rushing me."

"Also, it appears you've shit yourself."

It's a different story if Holly decides to change before leaving the house: I'm expected to critique four different outfits and take a photo of her modeling each with my phone so she can swipe-compare before making a final decision. After an argument over whether her shoes are blue-grey or grey-blue and the introduction of a fifth outfit, we'll finally leave and go wherever it was that we couldn't be late for and Holly will see herself in a window reflection on the way in and exclaim, "Oh my god. I can't believe you let me leave the house looking like this."

"You look fine."

"I wasn't going for fine. I was going for nice."

"You look nice."

"You can't just say it now. You've already established that I only look fine."

"Fine is better than nice. That's why they use it in front of art, furniture, and wine. Fine art is collectable, nice art is a framed print of a Picasso pencil drawing from IKEA."

"You're just backpedalling. It doesn't apply to what people are wearing. If you say someone's outfit is fine, that's just saying it will do. It will do isn't nice."

"What about fine apparel? Being dressed in fine apparel is a lot better than nice apparel."

"I'm not wearing fine apparel. I'm wearing Loft."

"And it's fine."

"Just so you know, your jacket and pants don't match and your hair looks terrible. It's very flat. Like you've been wearing a hat."

The Prodigy opened with *Voodoo People* and Keith Flint did a weird spasmodic dance between lyrics. There aren't a lot of lyrics in *Voodoo People* apart from "Voodoo people, who do what you don't dare do people," so it was mostly just spasmodic dancing. I wasn't familiar with the next couple of songs but everyone else seemed to know them. The crowd became an undulating wave of glow-sticks and Thomas performed a half-dance thing where he nodded and shook his fists like he was holding invisible maracas, but I just wasn't into it. My t-shirt was constricting, my legs hurt from standing, someone almost took my eye out with a glow-stick, and the music was kind of... annoying.

Thomas played me the album *The Fat of the Land* a few years later and I liked it enough to buy my own copy, but, at the time of the concert, The Prodigy's decent tracks like *Breathe*, *Smack My Bitch Up*, and *Firestarter* didn't exist. Most of the songs they played were just samples and boing noises. With spasmodic dancing. I felt out of place and awkward and, although I was only in my early twenties, everyone else there seemed half my age. I knew they were all wondering who the old man was and why he was there instead of at home in his Snuggie watching *Murder She Wrote*.

"I should have bought a notepad, Thomas."
"What for?"
"To take notes. That way everyone would think I was here doing a music review for a magazine."
"What the fuck are you talking about?"
"Never mind. Just go back to your invisible maracas."

There were ninety-four spotlights attached to the stage lighting rigs. I counted them. I wasn't sure if The Prodigy had played several songs after *Voodoo People*, or one really long song, but I hoped it was the former. Thirty minutes had passed since I'd taken the pill and I was bored and wasn't experiencing any effects, so I popped the second.

"I'm pretty sure that girl with the furry boots just sold you aspirin, Thomas. I had a headache earlier and it's gone but that's about it."
"They're not aspirin."
"Well I don't feel anything at all. Apart from bored and constricted."
"They can sometimes take a while to kick in."
"Maybe. Or maybe you got ripped off."
"Give it another twenty minutes and if you still don't feel anything, take the second one."
"I already took it."
"Really?"
"Yes. Was I not meant to?"
"No, you're meant to space them out a bit."
"Well that just reinforces my suspicions. I wish I had a couple more aspirin because my legs hurt. We should have paid for seat tickets - look at those people up there on the balcony, all comfortable and... Oooh, *Their Law*, I know this track. Did it just get warm in here? I feel like I'm melting. I should have worn thinner pants. Or my Adidas tennis shorts. They're sweat wicking. Did Keith Flint just stretch from one side of the stage to the other and then bounce back into his normal shape?"
"No. Why are you holding my hand?"
"So I don't lose you."

It was the best concert I've ever been to. It was loud and colourful and a girl wearing furry boots fell off a speaker and broke her arm. Keith stopped the music to ask if she was okay and gave a short speech about having fun but staying safe. Which was good advice. A short time before the accident, the girl that fell had played with my hair and given me several glow-stick bracelets to wear, which was nice of her. Everybody was very nice actually. There was a lot of hugging and face touching and it was just a very welcoming and positive environment to be in.

I made about forty new friends and Thomas had sex with a fat girl in the back of his Datsun after the concert. We gave her a lift home but her directions were vague and then she passed out so we left her at a bus stop.

"Did you have fun?"

"I did actually."

"See. You do need drugs to have fun."

"Sometimes. Not all the times though."

"Name one time that wouldn't be more fun on drugs."

"Swimming."

"In a race or just relaxing?"

"In a race."

"Fine. Name one more thing."

"Using a lathe."

"Fair enough. What have you got around your neck?"

"A necklace made out of glow-sticks."

"No, what are the lanyards with passes on them?"

"Oh, these? A guy named Peewee gave them to me. He said he liked my hat."

"What hat?"

"Just a hat. I don't have it anymore."

"When did all this happen?"

"While you were having sex with Starshaker. I went for a walk and helped Peewee carry a bunch of gear to his van."

"Stardancer, not Starshaker. What kind of gear?"

"Mixers and stuff."

"Peewee Ferris?"

"I think that was his name. How did you know?"

"He's the DJ that opened for The Prodigy. We missed most of his set because the t-shirt line was so long. What are the passes for?"

"Some kind of after party at Heaven nightclub. We should have gone to that instead of driving Starcrusher around in circles."

It was like the scene in movies where a car does a tire squealing 180° turn and hurtles back the way it came. Except the Datsun wasn't capable of spinning its wheels and it was a narrow road requiring a five-point turn.

I don't have a vivid memory of the after party but I remember it was loud and colourful and Keith Flint commented on how tight my t-shirt was. I didn't actually get to meet him but he pointed and laughed as he walked past with a big black guy and said, "Look how tight that guy's t-shirt is!"

A short time later the big black guy took away our passes and told us to leave because I was upsetting the other guests with my dancing.

I did meet Thomas's dad that night though. His name is Terry and he collects ceramic roosters. On our way home from the after party, Thomas stopped off at his parent's house to borrow an electric drill. I don't recall why we needed a drill but it probably wasn't for a carpentry project as it was three in the morning...

From: David Thorne
Date: Tuesday 5 March 2019 3.09pm
To: Thomas Harrer
Subject: Electric drill

Hello Thomas,

Keith Flint committed suicide yesterday and I'm writing a short article about the night we saw The Prodigy live.

I realize it was a while back, but after we left the after party, we stopped off at your parent's house to borrow an electric drill. It was the night Terry attacked me with a television aerial.

Do you remember what we needed the drill for?

David

From: Thomas Harrer
Date: Tuesday 5 March 2019 3.34pm
To: David Thorne
Subject: Re: Electric drill

That was almost 25 years ago.

How the fuck would I remember what we needed a drill for? All I remember is being thrown out of the party because you were showing everybody how Keith Flint dances and he saw you. And you were wearing a women's shirt.

Also, if I'm in the article, don't mention anything about drugs. Dad still reads your books even though he said the last couple were shit.

Thomas

....

I waited in the kitchen and looked around while Thomas went off in search of the drill. The kitchen cabinets stopped short a couple of feet from the ceiling and created a ledge on which sat approximately two hundred ceramic roosters of all shapes and sizes. One was pushing a wheelbarrow. I realise it's good to have a hobby but what makes one decide, "You know what? I've got a bit of time on my hands and I'm not that into stamps, I think I'll start a collection of ceramic roosters."?

It's not as if you can pass them down in your will or anything. Nobody is going to do a fist pump and exclaim, "Yes! Terry left me his dusty shelf roosters!"

They're going to be thrown out, Terry.

I suppose there are stupider things to collect. There must be. I know a guy named Mark who collects the pull-tabs from cans of Monster energy drinks, but at least once he has a thousand, he can trade them for a Monster backpack and beanie.

When I was young, I collected *Star Wars* action figures. They were the only presents I wanted for birthdays and Christmas, and I provided a list of all the action figures available, with the ones I already owned checked off, to my parents and relatives - just in case they were out shopping and happened to see a medical droid FX-7 action figure by chance. I wasn't collecting them as an investment, so I didn't keep them in their packaging, I displayed them in poses on three shelves grouped by Empire, Rebellion, and other. One of the action figures on the 'other' shelf was a Jawa (midgets in monk robes) wearing a vinyl cape. I had five other Jawa action figures, and their Sandcrawler, and none of those had vinyl capes. It kind of ruined my display and, figuring it was a cheap knock-off - not a real Kenner action figure - I threw it into my box of double-ups with the extra C3-POs, Boba Fetts and Han Solos. The only double-ups I kept on display were certain droids, the Jawas, and stormtroopers.

I had twenty stormtroopers, in two rows of ten, behind Darth Vader. There were a few more stormtroopers in my double-up box, but I was waiting until I had a full ten to make another row. Which is why I swapped my box of double-ups for seven stormtroopers with a kid named Fred Hickens after school one day. We weren't friends, we didn't like each other at all, but business is business.

Many years later, after I found out the vinyl caped Jawa was worth nearly fifty thousand dollars, I managed to track Fred Hickens down. He ran a mobile bug extermination business and his website included his email address. I emailed him asking if he still had the action figure by any chance and, if so, would he'd consider selling it for five hundred dollars. He reminded me who had come up with his nickname (Fried Chickens) and that he knew how much the action figure was worth because it had paid for his van. There's a moral in this, probably about schoolyard bullying. And yes, I realized about halfway through writing this tangent that it didn't support my argument about Terry's roosters.

I lit a cigarette while I waited for Thomas to get back with the drill. I'm not usually one to walk into someone's house and light a cigarette so I blame the pills entirely for the indiscretion. And for my decision to take off my t-shirt. It wasn't easy but I wiggled it up like a snake shedding its outer skin. The ripped sleeve seam finally gave out but the sleeve was tight and stayed on my upper arm like one of those arm things Cleopatra wore. The neck hole was difficult to get over my head so I left it around my forehead and swept the t-shirt back to complete the Egyptian look.

My freed skin felt like static mixed with felt and when I closed my eyes... I was hit with a television aerial. It was one of those 'rabbit ear' television aerials that have two long retractable metal stick things attached to a base, and it was more of a whipping weapon than a striking one. Most people have cable nowadays so you only ever see them in Wal-Mart or Dollar General stores. Some of them have a little plastic satellite dish on them to trick you into thinking you'll get transmissions from space.

"Look Evelyn, this television aerial has a little satellite dish on it. We should get that."
"We already have a television aerial."
"Yes, but ours doesn't have a satellite dish on it."
"What do we need a satellite dish for?"
"HBO."

In Terry's defense, he awoke to a noise and walked into his kitchen at 3AM to discover a topless stranger, possibly Egyptian, rubbing his torso while smoking a cigarette. He grabbed the nearest item at hand and attacked. The first lash across my back hurt the most - probably due to the contrast between experiencing near nirvana one moment and searing pain the next. The following lashes were also pretty bad but I was under a dining table by that time and most of the strikes were to my legs. I'm probably lucky Terry woke up before I decided to take off my pants. We were both yelling but Terry's yells were along the lines of, "Who are you?" and, "What are you doing in my house?" while mine were mainly, "Ow!" and, "Stop!"

The yelling brought Thomas in yelling and his mother joined us moments later. She was wielding a cordless telephone and declared that she'd dialed the first two numbers of the police and had her finger poised over the third. She must have seen this in a movie or something and was excited to put it into practice.

"Please tell your friend, for the third time, that nobody wants to feel his skin. Are you a gay, Thomas?"
"What? No."
"Well I can't say I approve of the company you keep. And why is he dressed like an Egyptian? He's making a spectacle of himself in public."

Thomas told me later that I wasn't welcome in his parent's house again because *A.* they thought I was a bad influence, and *B.* a ceramic rooster went missing. I was invited to a barbecue at their house a year or so later though; I figured Terry had put the incident behind him and was maybe even going to apologise for the beating. I made potato salad to take but then Thomas's parents told him they thought he'd meant the nice David from his work and I was uninvited. Which was pretty rude. If anyone deserves to hold a grudge from that night, it's me. I still have a long diagonal scar on my back from the vicious attack. And the ceramic rooster pushing a wheelbarrow. Whenever anyone asks me how I got it (the scar, not the rooster) I tell them I used to fence.

"But don't they have tips on the end of the swords to prevent such injuries, David?"
"Sure, but you can take them off pretty easy."
"Why would you want to?"
"Angry duels, that kind of thing. I'm not making it up. I have two trophies at home."

I do have two trophies at home so it's not a complete lie. One is for third place in a Spelling Bee when I was nine and the other is for 'longest streamer' in a kite-decorating contest. My design should have received the first prize of fifty dollars but they gave that to a Down syndrome kid for gluing a peacock feather onto a Batman kite.

I played *Their Law* for my offspring Seb in the car tonight. We were driving to Arby's because they have the meats. I don't have a subwoofer but I can turn the stereo all the way up to six before the speakers make a 'chhhhht' noise. Seb turned it down when we stopped at a red light because he didn't want the people in the car next to us to hear it.

"Not a fan?"
"No, not really. It's kind of... annoying."
"Yes, it really is. I think you have to be in the right frame of mind for it. They were good live though."

Speaker Testing at the Dodge Factory

"Is that as loud as it goes?"

"Yes, if you turn the dial to seven, the speakers go 'chhhht'. At eight they pop and have to be replaced."

"Perfect... I'll just make a tick on my clipboard... and you have a great day, Bob."

"You too, Roger."

"Oh, and Bob?"

"Yes?"

"Safety goggles?"

"It's casual Friday."

"That's not what it means, Bob. We've spoken about this."

Holly's Tortoise Joke

"Okay, so there's a turtle that lives in a house. No wait, three turtles. Actually they might be tortoises. Which are the ones that live a long time? Tortoises? Okay, three tortoises live in a house and one says, "We should have a picnic." No, hang on, I told it wrong. They all decide to go to the lake for a picnic. And you have to remember that tortoises live a long time. So the three tortoises go to the lake. They pack a picnic basket first. Then they go to the lake. It takes them fifty years to get to the lake, because they're tortoises. Then they realize they've forgotten the cheese so one of them agrees to go back and get it. A hundred years goes by and one of the tortoises says, "Harry will be back soon." The tortoise that went back to get the cheese is named Harry. Another hundred years goes by and a tortoise says, "Harry is taking a long time." Another hundred years goes by and one of the tortoises says, "I'm starving, let's just have a few crackers while we wait for Harry to get to back." That's what the cheese was for, crackers. So the tortoises start eating crackers and Harry jumps out of the woods and says, "I knew you'd start without me!" Oh wait, I forgot the important bit, Harry made the other two tortoises promise they wouldn't start the picnic without him. And they said they wouldn't. We should get a tortoise."

Safety Squirrel

I read about an African Grey parrot named Alex recently. As the name *African Grey parrot* implies, Alex was grey. Parrots, in general, are among the smartest birds in the animal kingdom, but the African Grey parrot is known for its ability to memorise names and phrases, and actually use them in context. Alex was particularly smart, even for an African Grey. He had a vocabulary of over 100 words, but was exceptional in that he displayed an understanding of what he said and could use words descriptively to express himself. His specialty was colours, of which he knew the names of many, and could identify them easily. When shown a banana, for example, and asked what colour it was, Alex would declare it was yellow. When shown a daffodil, Alex would describe it as light yellow. When asked if a green apple was purple, Alex would state, "No, the apple is green." His favourite colour was orange.

Alex was studied and tested by researchers constantly throughout his life. He lived to the ripe old age of thirty-one. During one session, just a few weeks before he stopped eating and passed away, Alex stared quietly at his own reflection in a mirror for several minutes and then asked, "What colour am I?"

I knew Spencer was transitioning but it had been six months since I'd last seen him. Her. It may take me a while to get used to using the correct pronoun - not because I'm being intentionally difficult, or because I have an issue with Spencer's decision, but because I've known her as him for so many years.

It was early spring the last time I saw Spencer. We were camping with a group of five or six other people at deer camp - my friend JM's family property in West Virginia. The property has a lot of trails and Spencer and I had spent the afternoon riding ATVs through the forest. The air was crisp and patches of snow still lay on the higher elevations, but trees were beginning to show green buds. We stopped at the top of a hill to have a cigarette and take in the view. Below and a few miles away, we could see smoke rising from the campsite.

Spencer had spent a couple of hours that morning chopping wood for the campfire while everyone else sat around telling him what a great job he was doing. The resulting pile was large enough to see us through the day and night. He enjoyed chopping wood. Or enjoyed the praise he received from chopping wood. Either way, he was good at it. While nobody would ever describe Spencer as muscular, at just over seven-feet and well over three hundred pounds, he had a lot of momentum behind his axe swings.

"Look, you can see the campsite from here, Spencer. Or at least the smoke."

"Oh yeah, someone must have put a wet log on the fire. I think I'll leave my helmet off on the ride back. It's 2XL but it's still giving me a headache."

"Safety Squirrel will be disappointed."

"Who's Safety Squirrel?"

"Just a squirrel that tells people he's disappointed when they're not being safe. It's a seventies thing. A guy in a squirrel costume visited Australian classrooms and showed kids a video. It never made a lot of sense to me because we don't have squirrels in Australia. He should have been Safety Snake or something."

"Then the person in the costume would have had to crawl everywhere."

"Good point. I can't think of any other Australian animals that begin with S though."

"What about Safety Shrimp? Shrimps are very Australian."

"Not really."

"What about 'throw a shrimp on the barbie'?"

"That was just tourism advertising for American audiences. We don't even call them shrimp in Australia. We call them prawns."

"Prudent Prawn then. Prudence is similar to safety."

"That's perfect. Prudent Prawn could visit schools and warn kids about the danger of touching hot surfaces."

"And water safety."

"Excellent point. Swimming is a part of Australian culture and I've never seen a squirrel swim."

"And bullying."

"Sure. Bullying isn't really a safety issue though."

"Of course it is. It's the second leading cause of death among young people aged ten to twenty-four and the numbers double when you're talking about the LGBT community."

"Are you just making these statistics up, Spencer?"

"No, I've researched it."

"Why?"

"Reasons."

Okay, fine. They'd probably need a different guy in a costume to talk to kids about bullying though. Maybe Empathy Emu. Prudent Prawn only covers issues like riding your bike at night without lights and asking a parent to help you use a sharp knife to cut sandwiches, not sexual orientation."

"You have no problem with LGBTs though, right?"

"No, I prefer gay people to the straight ones. Especially around here. I'd rather listen to techno than nonsense about Jesus, guns, and abortion clinics. I think there's something in the water. Maybe lead."

"Not all gay people like techno and not all LGBT people are gay. The T stands for transgender."

"Sure, but I assume a large percentage of transgender people are attracted to the same biological sex."

"Which would then make them straight."

"Yes, I suppose it would. I retract my statement."

"I want to be a woman."

"Yes, it would definitely be fun for a few hours. I'd take photos for later."

"No, I'm going to transition."

If I were a woman, I'd date one of the guys from the television show *Impractical Jokers*. They seem genuinely close so I'd effectively be getting four guys with a sense of humour for the price of one. It wouldn't matter too much which one I dated, as none of them are attractive, but the little skinny one with the bald head is definitely out. Dating him would be like dating a malnourished math teacher. Also the dark-haired old one looks a bit Armenian. Given a choice between dating the chubby one or the chubby one that wears hats, I'd have to go for the chubby one. I won't even sit in a meeting if my coworker Ben is wearing a hat. I had it written into my workplace agreement. If I were a woman, I'd date the chubby guy from the television show *Impractical Jokers*. Or a famous tennis player.

It was a brave decision for Spencer to make. The village we live in, Harrisonburg, has a small community of educated, open-minded people, and a larger community of people who watch *Fox News*. For every local who understands love is love, there's five raised pickup trucks with *Don't Step On a Snake* and *Trump 2020 - Make Liberals Cry Again* stickers on their rear windows. There's one particular matte-black pickup truck that has about twenty stickers and a giant Confederate flag attached to the back. I pulled up next to it at a set of traffic lights once and I could see the guy behind the wheel. He looked pretty much how I expected him to: Like someone that fucks young boys then kills them and buries the bodies behind his trailer so nobody learns his secret. Probably keeps the underpants though. As trophies.

In his glove box with the chambered .45 ACP handgun and tins of chewing tobacco. It takes all types though, that's what makes the world beautiful.

Harrisonburg does hold an annual Pride march, but it's usually just a handful of people waving rainbow flags and dodging beer cans thrown from passing pickup trucks. Someone caught a beer can last year and it made the local paper. The headline was '*Local shares beer with lesbian*'.

I chatted with Spencer several times over the next six months, mainly through Facebook Messenger. He told me he'd been taking hormones and his skin was softer but it can take two years to grow breasts so no, he wasn't going to send me a photo. He did send me a couple of links to outfits on Amazon and asked my opinion - I suggested black for its slimming effect but he had a preference for florals and pastels.

If I were a woman, I'd go for the horse-lady look: ponytail, jodhpurs, tall boots, and a vest. And I'd drive a Land Rover. I'd drive it into a paddock to look at my horses and my fiancé James would be with me and he'd tell me how great my butt looked in jodhpurs. Then we'd head home and change into our tennis gear.

I was sitting at my desk drinking coffee when I received the group email from Spencer stating he wished, from that point onwards, to be referred to as 'she' and that she had chosen a new name. I'd just taken a sip when I read the name and sprayed my desk and keyboard. Given the choice of any name, any name in the world, why would anyone choose *Sally*? If I were a woman, my name would be Jessica but my friends at the tennis club would call me Jess.

I knew a Sally in high school. She was a devout Christian and wore mom jeans to let everyone know. Mom jeans with huge pleats at the front. With white sneakers. She sat at the very front of class and answered questions like, "Can anyone tell me why sea water is salty?" with inane statements such as, "Because the Lord wept when Jesus was nailed to the cross."

Eventually the teacher just started telling Sally to put her hand down if her answer was going to be 'fucking stupid'.

"And can anyone tell me how rainbows are formed?"
"Ooh!"
"Anyone else apart from Sally?"
"Ooh!"
"Does your answer have anything to do with religion, Sally?"
"No."
"Nothing to with Jesus?"
"No."
"Fine, go ahead."
"God placed a rainbow in the clouds as a sign of his covenant with Noah and all the earth. *Genesis 9:13*."
"I specifically asked if your answer was about religion, Sally."
"It isn't. It's about the Ark."

I once flicked a piece of dog poo at Sally with a stick and it stuck to her crotch. In my defense, I didn't know the dog poo was soft inside and I wasn't aiming for her crotch. It was just a general flick. I was called to the principal's office a short time later and the principal made me apologise and sit in silence for several minutes while Sally prayed for me. It was a pretty big production for a bit of dog poo. It's not as if it went in her eye and blinded her or anything. There was a lot of adoration directed at the ceiling fan and referring to me as a 'sinner who knows not the error of his ways' and, after signing off with an 'Amen', she went in for a hug. I put my hand up to stop her and a finger accidently went up her nose and made it bleed. It was unintentional, but I still had to scrape chewing gum off the bottom of desks during lunch break.

A few weeks later, during a science project in which we each had to dissect a frog, Sally went to the bathroom and left her bag unattended. Without drawing attention to myself, I removed her lunch box, unwrapped the ham and cheese sandwich inside, placed my frog's lungs in it, and packaged it back up. Not my proudest moment but it was a spur of the moment decision and I thought it would be hilarious.

I hung around the schoolyard bench Sally ate at during lunch break, to ensure a good viewing position, and was brimming with anticipation as she unwrapped her sandwich and took a bite. A bit of the frog's spine must have still been attached because there was an audible crunch. Sally looked puzzled, but chewed and swallowed, then lifted the top slice of bread to look inside. Then closed it and took another bite.

I actually saw a section of lung stretch from the sandwich, like melted cheese on a pizza, so it's not as if she'd eaten the majority with the first bite and hadn't seen any goopy bits when she peered inside. Perhaps she thought it was some kind of chutney her mother had added that morning. Perhaps frog lungs are delicious. Regardless, it was anticlimactic and disappointing. Without a negative reaction, the whole exercise was made pointless and I considered, for a moment, yelling, "Haha, you ate frog lungs, and maybe a bit of spine, in your sandwich."

I'm lucky I didn't because Sally was rushed to hospital less than an hour later. She was a weird bluish-green colour, covered in vomit and sweat, shaking uncontrollably, and had shit herself. As the ambulance medics wheeled her out of class, she sobbed, "Don't look at me."

I've had 'standard' food poisoning before and it was five or six hours after I'd eaten, so whatever bacteria or toxin the frog's lungs contained must have been quite an aggressive strain. I'd noticed, while we dissected the frogs, mine had more slimy bile inside it than some of the others, so maybe that had something to do with it. I'd mentioned the bile to the teacher at the time and he told me, "They've just been out of the freezer too long - we were meant to do this project last week. Just mop it up a bit with a paper towel."

I felt terrible. And scared. Not for Sally, for myself. She wasn't at school the next day, or the day after. By the third day, I was convinced she had died and forensic scientists were analyzing the contents of Sally's stomach and would, at any moment, declare, "Ah. Frog lungs... and we have a fingerprint on one of them."

Sally returned to school the following week. She looked pale and had lost a lot of weight, but apparently Jesus had held her hand throughout the whole ordeal and told her, "It's not your time, child."

"So you actually saw Jesus?"
"Yes."
"Did he say anything about frogs?"
"No, why?"
"No reason."

I saw Sally several years later during an arts festival called *The Adelaide Fringe*. It's an annual month-long event, with performances and live music, targeted at lesbian social workers that wear fair-trade scarves. It's the kind of thing I usually avoid as I'm not a huge fan of potato-flute solos or poetry readings about underarm hair. I'd only agreed to attend a play called *Something's Wrong with Steven* because a friend of mine, Bill, was dating Steven - the writer, director and star. Steven may have also been the stage designer as the set consisted of a green vinyl kitchen chair, a giant knife made out of cardboard and aluminium foil, and a bucket.

It was a dreadful play, without dialogue, and was about an hour too long. Steven, the titular character, sat on a chair naked for the entire performance while several people circled him yelling and screaming. For an hour. I went out for a cigarette halfway through, and fell asleep for several minutes towards the end, but I don't think I missed any integral plot development. At the end of the play, Steven stood, tap-danced barefooted for ten minutes, pretended to cut his wrists with the giant knife made out of cardboard and aluminium foil, and poured a bucket of blood over his head.

"Well that was pretty good, Bill. Thank you for inviting me."
"Is that sarcasm?"
"Not at all. My favourite part was the screaming. I'm glad Steven was able to get us front row tickets."
"Maybe you just didn't understand the metaphor because you're straight."
"Yes, probably. It was rather subtle. I hope this is fake blood, some went in my mouth. They should have given us plastic ponchos like they do at Seaworld. You owe me a new shirt regardless."
"Looks good, let's go."
"You're not going to wait for Steven?"
"No, he has to take a shower and needs a few hours to come down from each performance. It takes a lot out of him."
"I'm sure it does, I sat in a chair for the same amount of time as he did and I'm mentally drained. Plus he did a dance."
"It's easy to be critical. I doubt you'd be capable of sitting motionless for an hour without flinching while people

scream at you."

"Please, that's a normal hour at the office for me... Oh my God, that's Shitpants Sally. I went to high school with her."

A small group of protestors were picketing outside the venue. Apparently they had an issue with Steven's play and knew holding signs while singing *Go Tell It On the Mountain* would fix everything. Sally's sign, a pizza box decorated with poster paint, declared, "If there is a man who lies with a male as those who lie with a woman, both of them have committed a detestble act. *Leviticus 201:13*"

"You spelled detestable wrong."

"Yes, I'm aware of that, thank you. Would you like a pamphlet that answers any questions you may have about homosexuality?"

"No thank you, I don't have any questions. Do you remember me, Sally? We were in the same class at school. I flicked dog poo onto your crotch."

"David? Yes, I remember you."

"Do you remember the day we dissected a frog in science class and you became violently ill a short time later and shit your pants and were taken away in an ambulance?

"Yes, I almost died."

"That's because I put my dissected frog's lungs in your ham and cheese sandwich. And maybe a bit of its spine. I watched you eat the sandwich and then an hour later you were taken to the hospital. Well, it was really nice seeing you again, Sally."

If we confess our sins, he is just to forgive and to cleanse us from all unrighteousness.

James 5:16

I was fifteen minutes early to pick up Sally. It would be the first time I saw her as a woman and I was probably more nervous than she was. I was worried I'd laugh or say something stupid, something hurtful, something that might change Sally's mind about going to deer camp for the weekend. It made sense that deer camp would be Sally's first public outing, it was an environment she felt comfortable in, an environment where she would know everyone. I paused at the front door, took a deep breath, and knocked.

I knew Sally had lost a lot of weight as she'd posted several hundred photos of her bathroom scales over the previous six months. The last had read 170 pounds which is less than I weigh and quite extraordinary for her height. I hit 200 pounds recently and was told to cut cheese and bread from my diet and exercise regularly, so I'm going to get fat. I'll blame my thyroid or a dicky knee from the time I stood up without realizing my leg was asleep and it bent backwards.

Despite Sally's impressive bathroom scale numbers, I was still kind of expecting 'Spencer in a dress'. It's why I was apprehensive about my reaction. I've seen tall drag queens in brightly coloured wigs and exaggerated makeup, so it's possible that image tinged my expectations. They're only a step up from clowns and I'm not a huge fan of clowns.

Especially fast clowns. I went to a friend's birthday party when I was five or six and he had a fast clown there making balloon animals and hats. I asked the clown for a balloon hat and he made me a sausage dog. When I complained, he grabbed my arm really fast, squeezed hard enough to hurt, and said, "I don't give a fuck what you want kid, take the fucking sausage dog."

I intended to tell an adult but when I approached the birthday boy's mother, the clown appeared out of nowhere, grinned menacingly at me, and asked loudly, "Do you like your sausage dog?" and I replied, "Yes, thank you."

I realize it's not much of a frightening clown story but it's my frightening clown story. More of an arsehole clown story than a frightening one really. Still, fuck clowns. It was a long time ago but if I knew who that clown was and he was still working, I'd leave a bad review on Yelp. I think his name was Barry.

Sally didn't look like a clown or a drag queen. Or like 'Spencer in a dress'. Her hair, dyed blue-black and straightened, was cut into a sleek bob that fell just below her shoulders. Her makeup was understated and flawless. She wore a simple orange summer dress with roman sandals and her toenails were painted to match the dress. As a man, Spencer was probably a 3, maybe a 4 in good lighting. As a woman, Sally was a solid 17.

My scaling system goes to 25, so not exactly gorgeous, but if someone pointed Sally out in a bar, and you were single and had been drinking Long Island Iced Teas all night, and she was sitting in a booth so you couldn't tell how tall she was, you might nod and say, "Yeah, not bad."

"You're fifteen minutes early."

"Wow. You scrub up well."

"It's not too much?"

"Not at all. I was worried you might look like a clown but you definitely don't."

"Why would I look like a clown?"

"If you'd gone with lots of makeup and green hair or something."

"And a red nose?"

"No, that's just being silly. I meant more like a drag queen."

"I look like a drag queen?"

"No, I was worried you might but you look fine."

"Just fine?"

"Why does everyone have a problem with the word fine? You look nice. I like the dress."

"It's from the Tory Burch summer collection. Toucan Floral. It's actually meant to go all the way down to the ankles but I don't mind that it shows my calves. You really think I look nice?"

"Very nice. If was single and saw you in a bar, and I didn't know you had a penis..."

"Yeah, you're not my type. But thank you."

"What's that supposed to mean?"

"Sorry?"

"What's 'not my type' meant to mean?"

"Physically you're not my type."

"Why? Are you saying I'm fat? I have a thyroid."

"You're not fat, you just have a bit of a belly."

"Nice. I retract my partial statement about the pub then."

"Too late. I already know you want to fuck me."

"That's not what I said. If you had let me finish, I was going to say, 'If someone pointed you out, I'd nod and say, "Yeah, not bad."'"

"That's still pretty good."

"Yes, it is. You're definitely a solid 17."

"Out of what? 20?"

"Sure."

"Using what scaling system? What's a 1?"

"I don't know, maybe Sméagol."

"The cave guy from *Lord of the Rings*?"

"He's very unattractive. I had a dream about him chasing me with scissors once."

"What's a 20?"

"Probably Anne Hathaway. I have a thing for big faces."

During the two-hour drive from Harrisonburg to deer camp in West Virginia, we drank quad-shot breve lattes from Starbucks, listened to techno music, discussed the price of women's haircuts, and argued about pizza toppings. The whole anti-pineapple bias gets a bit old and I'm pretty sure people just pretend to dislike pineapple on pizza because it's a thing and people like to be a part of things.

"Oh, you can't stand pineapple on pizza? No problem, I'll put caterpillars on yours instead."

"Why would I want caterpillars on my pizza?"

"It's a choice between caterpillars or pineapple I'm afraid."

"I'll have pineapple then."

"Yes, I thought as much, bigot."

"Well the alternative was a bit extreme."

"Fine. Pineapple or meat?"

"What kind of meat?"

"Caterpillar."

There were seven people waiting for us at camp - JM, his sons Joseph and Andrew, Brandon the vape oil expert, Cody the human slug, Mark the non-practicing Jew, and Kyle the truck mechanic. They were all wearing dresses and JM and Joseph had on wigs even though wigs hadn't been mentioned in the group email. Some people just have to be the centre of attention. I changed into a blue Sixties style mod dress I'd bought the day before at TJ Maxx - I'd looked for a pair of knee-high boots to go with the dress but the closest TJ Maxx had was rubber rain boots so I just bought the dress, soaps, candles, a bottle of olive oil with a sprig of rosemary in it, and a ceramic owl.

Sally was pleased with the effort and did the 'fanning her eyes' thing with her hands so she wouldn't cry and mess up her makeup. There were hugs and everyone exclaimed how amazing she looked and made jokes about sleeping arrangements and sitting down to use the toilet.

Mark seemed particularly impressed with Sally and commented after a few beers that he'd definitely fuck her. Sally didn't tell him that he wasn't her type, which annoyed me a bit. Mark likes to think he looks like Vin Diesel but he actually looks more like a large dwarf baby with partial Down syndrome. He's somehow quite popular with the ladies though. Homeless ladies without teeth mainly. They use the free Wi-Fi at Starbucks, after stealing all the sugar sachets, to swipe right on Mark's Tinder profile photo of him holding cans of food. That's not to say Mark is without standards, he hoses down his dates in the driveway before they're allowed inside.

After the excitement of Sally's debut had calmed down, things went back to normal in camp. We drank beer, Sally chopped wood for the fire, Mark watched her, JM complained about Mexicans stealing his corn, Joseph whittled a spoon, Andrew showed us how to do the Floss, Kyle explained why Scania trucks aren't all they're cracked up to be, Brandon argued that Aquaman would beat The Flash if they fought in a really heavy downpour, and Cody sat in a chair struggling to breath. Occasionally someone poked him with a stick to check he was still alive.

I pitched my tent and unloaded the ATVs so that Sally and I could go for a ride.

The trail leading up the valley was carpeted with orange and yellow leaves and many of the trees were already bare. It was still warm enough to ride in just a dress, but a cool breeze hinted that winter was just around the corner and I was glad I had on cargo shorts underneath. We stopped on top of a hill to have a cigarette and take in the view. Below and a few miles away, we could see smoke rising from the campsite.

"Look, you can see the campsite from here, Spencer."

"Sally."

"Sorry. Sally. It may take me a while. As you could have chosen any name, any name in the world, why Sally?"

"My parents gave me a monogrammed towel set a few years ago so I thought I should stick with a name that starts with an S."

"Are you serious?"

"They're nice towels."

"I knew a Sally in high school."

"Was she nice?"

"Sure."

"That's good. I think I'll leave my helmet off on the ride back. It's messing up my hair and I paid nearly two-hundred dollars for the colour and cut."

"Caution Crocodile will be disappointed."

"I thought we'd settled on Prudent Prawn?"

"It's too matronly. Nobody uses the word prudent. I just picture a prawn dressed as Mary Poppins."

"It's better than Caution Crocodile. That just sounds like a sign warning people not to swim."

That evening, well after the fire had died down and everyone had retired for the night, Mark crept into Sally's tent. There was a bit of a scuffle and Mark ended up with a split lip. He claimed he'd gotten up during the night to urinate and had mistaken Sally's tent for his own on his way back to bed, but this seems unlikely; Sally's tent is a green and blue Coleman four-person dome tent with fairy-lights strung around the entrance, while Mark's tent is a canvas painter's drop-cloth draped over the bed of his raised pickup truck and held in place by duct-tape.

The Harrisonburg annual Pride march was held last week. There was a decent turnout this year with the number of participants doubling to ten. Sally, dressed as a mermaid for no conceivable reason, smiled and waved excitedly to us as she rode down Main Street on her rented Lime® electric scooter. She was wearing a helmet so Diligent Dingo would have approved.

A small group of protesters stood on the sidewalk holding signs about Jesus, but they left after someone threw a can of beer at them.

More Bridges

21. In eighth grade, Steven Butcher demonstrated how to perform cunnilingus by sticking his tongue in a condom he found at a bus stop.

22. Peter Stevens backed his car over his sister's cat in his driveway. His sister was away at a netball competition at the time. When she returned, Peter feigned ignorance as to the cat's whereabouts and his sister spent two days putting up lost posters. Renee, if you're reading this, I tried to convince Peter a burial was appropriate, but he chose to double-wrap Oscar in a garbage bag and put him out with the trash. It was a quick death if that helps, Oscar's head was crushed. That's what the dark stain on the driveway is, Renee, not a dropped bottle of Sauvignon Blanc as Peter claimed.

23. In fifth grade, Jason Bartling took a dump in a mop bucket because he didn't think he'd make it to the bathroom. He cried while he did it because everyone was watching him. I felt sorry for him at the time but then he took a dump on the floor of a school bus a few weeks later and Peter Jackson (not the director) threw my schoolbag onto Jason's poo.

24. In sixth grade, Martin Kelly told everyone his dad had died in a car crash. We held a minute of silence for Mr Kelly at school assembly. A week later, at the next assembly, Mr Kelly made Martin apologise to the whole school for telling lies.

25. Melissa Peters once gave herself a promotion and raise without anyone realizing for six months. She also purchased a three thousand dollar massage chair and a parrot on the company credit card.

26. Eric Henley photoshopped himself into a photo of a random girl he found online and told everyone she was his long-distance girlfriend named Sarah. He kept the framed photo on his desk for over a year until the movie *X-Men: First Class* came out and everyone realised the girl in the photo was Jennifer Lawrence.

27. Mitchell Warner asked the teacher, in the middle of a sixth grade geography class, if the stuff that comes out of your penis when you rub it is poisonous.

28. Ben Townsend came into my office last week and bent over my desk to point at something on my monitor. I asked if him if he'd mind not sticking his stinky bum in my face and he replied, "My bum isn't stinky. It's perfectly clean. When I shower, I lather my finger up with soap and stick it in as far as it will go. I bet you don't do that."

29. In ninth grade, Louise Mackay told Mr Robinson, our gym teacher, that she loved him and hoped that his wife died in a car accident. He told her this was inappropriate and sent her to the principal. The next day, Louise smeared dog poo on Mr Robinson's car windows and was suspended for a week. The day she came back, she hid under Mr Robinson's car and he ran over her leg.

30. Tracey Williams is an alcoholic. Check her middle desk drawer. Behind the pen and paperclip boxes. There might be some weed in there as well.

31. Daniel Johnston crashed his father's Nissan through a fence while his father was away on business. He then caught a bus home and reported the vehicle stolen. In his defence, he'd taken a lot of ecstasy and swerved when he thought the lines painted on the road were lazers being shot at him.

32. Richard Halterman Photoshops the faces of females he's friends with on Facebook onto nude photos from porn sites. He has a folder on his laptop called *FBFriends2019* containing over four hundred images. A quick search of his recent Internet search history also reveals he likes Ford Mustang convertibles, pleated non-wrinkle work pants, and "Girls that are asleep."

Stalactites

Laura was expecting guests for dinner and the house was a mess. The sink was stacked with dirty dishes to the point where they had overflowed to the countertop and stove surface - somewhere under the dishes were food scraps and a smelly sponge caked in cheese sauce from a meal she'd made weeks before. Flies and ants crawled over everything, congregating around empty food cans and Ramen noodle cups. A cockroach scuttled across the kitchen floor, stopped to investigate a congealed puddle of cat vomit, moved on to an oily slice of cheese. The vent above the stove was caked in an inch-thick layer of grease and dust - its weight had caused clumps to hang down like stalactites, or perhaps stalagmites, I'm not sure which is which because I'm not a cave expert. I think the way to remember how to tell them apart is 'you *might* trip over a stalag*mite* but the stalactites are stuck *tight* to the ceiling' but I can't recall if I read this somewhere or made it up.

It was 6.45pm. The guests would arrive in fifteen minutes but Laura had it all under control. She locked the door, turned off the lights, and crawled into bed. "Goodnight kitty kitty, you're so pretty," she whispered, stroking the cat next to her. It had been dead for three weeks.

Hugs Are Always Nice

I learned, just this week, that my mother died a few months ago. Her name was Diane. I'm not sure how I'm meant to feel about her death, as we weren't close. Writing '*was* Diane' instead of '*is*' caused me to pause for a moment, but it was a brief moment. I've felt more emotion watching television commercials for St. Jude's Children's Hospital even though I've worked in advertising and know exactly how it all works.

"Can someone swap this child for a more attractive one please? Preferably one that's able to smile on cue despite the pain. Is that really too much to ask?"
"How about this one?"
"No, she's not bald enough. And she's Mexican. Nobody in America wants to see Mexican kids getting free cancer treatment. We might stick a black kid in somewhere for legal reasons, but only one and it has to be from a talent agency. We can shave its head if we need to, it's in their contract."
"What about this one? He's white, completely bald, and the pain from eighteen bone marrow transplants has contorted his face into a permanent smile."
"Fine, he'll do. Just stick a few more tubes up his nose and give him a colouring book. I don't want to be here all day, it's fucking depressing."

A death in the family does tend to make you think about your own mortality though. That and accidently looking at the X10 side of a bathroom magnifying mirror. I looked at the magnified side of one the other day, while Holly and I were in Bed Bath & Beyond shopping for new sheets, and I've decided I'm never standing within twenty feet of anyone ever again. Before that moment, I believed I looked 'somewhere in my early forties' but the magnified mirror informed me I could pass for Walter Matthau's dad. It also let me know that there was a thick black hair, approximately a centimetre long, growing out of one of the manhole sized pores in my nose.

"Holly, there's a thick black hair growing out of my nose."
"Yes, it's hard to miss."
"What? How long has it been there?"
"I don't know, six months."
"And you didn't think to mention it?"
"I figured you'd seen it."
"And what, I decided to keep it? To see how long it would get? Why would I do that?"
"Who knows why you do half the things you do."

Along with, "Looks good, let's go," and, "Will you rub my back?", the phrase, "Who knows why you do half the things you do," is an integral multi-use tool in Holly's repertoire. It serves as dismissal, insult, justification, and accusation reinforcement.

"Where's the measuring cup gone? Have you seen it?"

"No, Holly."

"Did you throw it out?"

"Why would I throw out the measuring cup?"

"Who knows why you do half the things your do."

"That's just your go-to response when you have no basis for the accusation."

"Past behaviour is the basis. You threw out the wooden Christmas nativity my parents gave us last year."

"Yes, because we're atheists. Why the fuck would we want a wooden nativity scene in our house? It's as if your parents purposely seek out the tackiest rubbish they can find at Dollar General in an effort to fuck with our interior design choices and turn our house into Grandma Bumpkin's trailer in the woods. They gave us a ceramic statue of a bear with a butterfly on its nose the year before. I threw that out as well. And the sofa pillow with Nascar driver Dale Earnhardt Jr.'s face on it."

"They mean well."

"I'm sure they do. They probably thought, 'You know what would go well with David and Holly's Mid-Century Modern furniture? A Nascar pillow. Neither of them have the slightest interest in Nascar but everyone loves tassels.' The next time they give us something dreadful, I'm just going to say, 'No, sorry, that's not going in our house, it's hideous and I hate it.'"

"Why would you do that?"

"Who knows why I do half the things I do, Holly."

"You weren't hugged much as a child, were you?"

I ran away from home when I was five. I didn't like being there and I knew of a much better house where lots of kids lived - a couple of the kids were around my age. I wasn't sure of the address but I knew what the front of the house looked like because I'd seen it dozens of times. Our house was a place where you had to be quiet and weren't allowed to touch anything. A house of good behaviour. The house I was running away to was full of life and laughter - there was a seesaw in the backyard and the family did fun activities together, such as sack racing. I knew there was a spare bed for me in Peter and Bobby's room because Greg, the oldest brother, had recently moved into the attic.

I only made it four or five blocks before Mr Kostas, our Greek neighbour, drove past and stopped to ask where I was off to and if I wanted a lift. Apparently he didn't watch a lot of television because we drove around for half an hour or so looking for the Brady house before he took me home. Or perhaps he was just humouring me. We did stop to pick up several bags of concrete and some rebar from a hardware store on the way and he told me a story about how his mother used to whip him with an olive tree branch when he got poor grades at school.

I assume there was a funeral for Diane, I wasn't told. Probably because whoever arranged it, most likely my sister Leith, knew I wouldn't attend. Or she didn't want to split the proceeds from the sale of Diane's house. I don't care. She needs the money more than I do. It can't be easy raising five kids from five different fathers who are all either in prison or gave false names and addresses and can't be located.

"Who's my dad?"
"Lamp Couch Hallway. He had brown hair just like yours."
"Will I ever meet him?"
"No, he's an astronaut and lives on the moon. Hush now, finish your 1/5th of the Big Mac then get ready for bed. It's your turn to have the blanket tonight."
"Yay!"

I once lent my sister five hundred dollars, to fix the transmission on her van, and she bought an above ground pool. I never saw a cent of the money again and I never went for a swim because, well, it was an above ground pool. Even if you build a deck around one everyone knows what it is. Nobody says, "Oh really? It's an above ground pool? You'd never be able to tell." They say, "Oh, the invite didn't mention it's an above ground pool. I wouldn't have come if I'd known." Maybe not to your face but that's what they're saying. Leith didn't have a deck around her pool so everyone just sat in Coleman camping chairs looking up at it. I mentioned the money a few years later and Leith stated, "I bought you a pool float."

I don't even know how Diane died. She was only in her sixties and did Pilates so maybe it was an illness or an automobile accident. I hope it was quick because in the end, that's all any of us can hope for. A quick death, sometime in my seventies, is basically my retirement plan. I don't care how I die as long as it's quick and has nothing to do with sharks. I know a guy named Jason that used to work as an EMT and he told me that a surprisingly large amount of people die on the toilet. Apparently pushing out a big poo puts the cardiovascular system at risk by raising blood pressure, increasing the risk of a stroke or heart attack. I'm at that age where I can have a stroke or drop dead at any time so I always make sure my hair is done and I'm wearing clean underwear before I take a dump. I also cover my genitals with a towel and make sure my browser history has been deleted.

Apparently Diane was quite good looking when she was young but I've seen photos of her in a marriage album and I never thought so. Perhaps because she wasn't smiling in any of them. I saw Diane smile three times when I was growing up. I'm sure she smiled more often than that and I've just forgotten, but that's all I can recall. Once was when Gravox sent her two pallets of tins of instant gravy after she cut her thumb on a lid and wrote them a scathing letter, once during the telecast of Prince Charles and Lady Diana's wedding, and once when my father fell out of a boat. The boat was on a trailer and my father broke his arm.

All three smiles occurred before my father left. It's possible she smiled when I was a baby but I don't remember much before the age of five so I have no idea when she realized she never should have married my father and had children.

Diane wasn't a terrible mother, she went through the motions, but it was a fairly transparent performance in a role that bought her no joy. It was the 'movie adaption of a book' version of motherhood that omitted certain dialogue and character development in order to fit within the ninety-minute runtime audiences are comfortable with. But made for television. On a budget. With an actor you know you've seen in something else but can't quite put your finger on it. It might have been that show about rescue helicopter pilots.

I was eleven when I had my first sleepover at a friend's house. I know that's old to be having your first sleepover but my mother didn't like other kids at our house because we had an expensive rug or something, I think it was Berber, and sleeping at other kid's houses involved being dropped off and picked up and the possibility of her having to talk to other parents. It was a lot of work.

"Mum, can I sleep over Michael Wilson's house?"
"Who's Michael Wilson?"
"My best friend from school. You don't have to do anything."
"Have I met Michael?"
"Not yet."
"Then no. What would people think? For all I know his father might be a child rapist."
"He's not. He's a washing machine mechanic."
"Definitely not then. Are they poor?"
"No. They have a pool."
"Above ground or inground?"

Michael and I had pizza for dinner and played *Missile Command* on his Atari until his mother told us to go to sleep for the fourth or fifth time. Before Michael's mother turned out the light, she held open her arms and Michael embraced her in a tight hug. It lasted several seconds. "Goodnight pumpkin," she said, "See you in the morning." It was weird. Was it some kind of ritual they had? Like saying grace or picnics? I should have been warned... Michael's mother smiled at me and held her arms out. I froze like a deer caught in headlights. Was I supposed to hug Michael's mum? Who goes around hugging other people's chil... She grabbed me and held me tight, rocking side to side. Her fluffy pink robe was warm and smelled like apple laundry detergent. "Goodnight, David," she said, "See you in the morning."

I rode my bike home the next day, before lunch as agreed. My mother was on the couch in our living room watching daytime television. I approached her with my arms out like an idiot. It was something new but I'd decided to go for it. She asked what I was doing and I explained I was giving her a hug.

"Why? Were you molested?"
"No."
"What's wrong then?"
"Nothing."
"Well I'm sure it can wait until the commercial break then. *Coronation Street* is on and Billy just confronted Deidre about her affair with Baldwin."

You couldn't pause television in those days. There was no such thing as 'on demand' or even any way to record programs. If you missed something, too bad, wait for the re-run in four or five years. It made the punishment of not being allowed to watch television after dinner if you'd done something wrong an actual punishment. You'd hear about all the exciting things that happened in that night's episode of *Quantum Leap* from kids at school the next day and wish your parents were dead. If I were to tell my offspring that he wasn't allowed to watch a program on television, he'd just say, "Fine, I'll watch it online later." Likewise with being sent to your room. When I was sent to my room as a kid, there was nothing to do so I'd just lie on my bed being angry and wait. My offspring has cable television, gaming consoles, a smartphone, and a computer in his room. The only way to punish him is to turn off the Wi-Fi hub. Once, when he was being particularly annoying, I took the hub with me on an overnight work trip. He sent me furious messages for a couple of hours but eventually ran out of data on his phone.

My mother held me awkwardly, lightly, like one might politely embrace a distant relative at a function. There was no rocking side to side or apple scented warm fluffy pink robe. After a few seconds she patted my back and said, "Okay, that's enough, you're blocking the television and I haven't seen this advertisement for paper towels."

It was the first time I ever remember hugging my mother. Or my mother hugging me. The second time we awkwardly hugged was many years later at my grandfather's funeral. I worked out what was wrong though, what was missing, why her mechanical anxious hug wasn't the same as the safe calming hug from Michael's mother. Mother's Day was just a few weeks away and I convinced my father to take me to K-mart.

"Happy mother's day!"
"A pink robe?"
"Yes. You should put it on."
"I don't wear pink. And I don't wear polyester. Did you keep the receipt? I'll exchange it for an ironing board cover."

I realize at this point you're probably saying to yourself, "Oh, poor David. Mummy didn't give you hugs. My mother made me work at a gloryhole when I was six and sold me to gypsies when I was ten," but I'm getting to the fucked up bit and this isn't about you.

My father had twelve affairs that I know of. I'm sure there were more. For years it seemed like there was a new one every couple of months. They were always with wives of friends and the affair always came out and my parents would sit with the other couple in our backyard 'talking it out'. My sister and I often listened through the bathroom window, giving each other wide-eyed looks as sexual encounters were described in detail and voices became raised. Once, my father was punched in the nose and he had to go to hospital.

By the seventh or eighth affair we didn't bother listening at the window, we'd heard it all before and knew to be quiet for a few weeks and then things would go back to normal. But one time it didn't. Maybe it was because the affair was with my mother's best friend, Rosemary. Maybe it was because my father didn't just brush it off as 'a mistake that shouldn't have happened' like he usually did, but instead said he had feelings for Rosemary. That he loved her and she felt the same.

I was sitting in the front seat of our station wagon, Leith was in the back. My mother had told us to quickly pack a bag of clothes and get in the car. My father tried to stop her leaving but he didn't try very hard. I think the cricket was on. I don't know where my mother was planning to take us, or if she even knew. Maybe she intended to work that out while she was driving. Ten or fifteen minutes from our house, my mother turned onto an open stretch of road that went all the way to the next town. It was mostly straight and surrounded by farmland and gum trees. Sometimes my friend Michael and I rode our bikes there because a side road led to a pond with turtles in it.

I noticed we were speeding and asked my mother to slow down. She looked at me, looked in the rear-vision mirror at my sister, then pushed the accelerator pedal to the floor. I remember my sister yelling and the engine screaming, and my mother, expressionless, purposely turning the steering wheel to head towards a large gum tree.

We must have been travelling a hundred miles per hour when we left the road. The car slid and dirt and gravel pelted the windows. My mother wrestled with the steering wheel, but she had no control at that point. We missed the target gum tree, glanced off a second, and hit a third. It wasn't a head-on crash; the glance from the second tree had spun the car enough to take a drivers-side impact. It had also slowed us down somewhat and, although the vehicle was a complete write-off, there were no life-threatening injuries. My mother broke her left wrist and Leith suffered superficial cuts to her face from a shattered rear window, but I only received bruises and a realization. Or maybe confirmation of a realization I'd had years before.

Diane stated in the accident report that she was going the speed limit and had attempted to steer around an animal on the road. I think she said it was a chicken. I didn't see any chicken though.

A few months after the accident, my father ran off with the lady who did the member's fees and match scheduling at his tennis club. They eventually married and, fifteen years later, she cheated on him with a security guard named Gary. I didn't see Diane much after my father left. The transparent performance was no longer necessary and there was a lock on her bedroom door. My sister and I survived on tomato soup and I left home when I was fourteen. Leith had her first kid to guy named Jeans Socksandkeys around that time and moved into a caravan in a field.

When I told Holly that Diane had died, she said she was sorry and that it was okay to cry, and asked if I wanted her stay home from work. I didn't need her to stay home or apologise for the death of a woman I hardly knew. And I didn't cry. The last time I cried was when a squirrel I rescued died. I bawled my eyes out for hours and I still miss him years later. Sure, he was a pretty awesome squirrel, but the fact that a rodent's death had more impact on me than my mother's should be a pretty clear indicator of the fucks I give. Holly gave me a hug anyway, which was nice. Hugs are always nice.

I walked down the hallway to Seb's bedroom a few minutes ago. He was playing *League of Warcraft* on the gaming machine he recently built. 75% of Seb's days are spent playing *League of Warcraft*, with the remaining 25% split between sleeping and microwaving Hot Pockets. I gave him a big hug, with side-to-side action, and he asked me what the hug was for.

"Nothing," I told him, "I just love you."
"Gay," he replied, "Shut the door on your way out, I'm streaming to two-hundred people and I'm in ranked and on my promotional divisions."

I have no idea what any of that meant but it was a bit rude so I switched off the Wi-Fi.

The Exciting
Adventures of Seb

Walter's Whining

If complaining was an Olympic sport, my coworker Walter would be on the front of Wheaties boxes. He'd whine about the photo they chose and tell everyone he actually sent Wheaties a better photo to use but they went with the one he didn't like. The one where his hair sticks up at the back. How hard would it have been to Photoshop it a bit?

I enjoy a good whine myself but I'm not in Walter's class. Walter whines about the colour of doorknobs, the stickiness of sticky tape, the size of buttons on calculators, the weight of pens, the elasticity of rubber bands, the slipperiness of soap... At least fifty percent of Walter's working day is spent whining. I've no idea what percentage of his non-working time is spent whining because there's no way I'd hang out after hours with someone who whines so much.

This morning, while Walter was whining about the thickness of the froth in his latte, I asked, "Do you ever stop whining?" and he replied, "What are you talking about? I never whine. I'm the most easy-going guy on the planet."

As such, I've decided to make a record of every time Walter whines today:

9.23am

"How loud is this light switch? Listen to it. That's the loudest click I've ever heard. There's no need for it to be that loud."

9.38am

"I know someone's been sitting at my desk because I never have my chair this high. It's rude to change someone else's chair height. Maybe I'll just walk around and change everyone else's chair height and see how they like it."

9.44pm

"Did the cleaner empty your waste bin? She didn't empty mine. I know because there's a banana peel in it and I haven't had a banana since Monday."

9.50am

"What's wrong with this window? Who makes a window like this? What are these stupid plastic triangle stopper things even for? Guess I'm just not allowed to have fresh air today."

10.17am

"How am I meant to work with that bird making so much noise? Can you hear it? I think it's a pigeon."

10.24am

"What's wrong with the Internet today?"

10.38am

"My shirt is itchy. I think I might be allergic to Gain laundry detergent. Just the Island Fresh Flings though. The original scent Gain doesn't make me itchy."

10.52am

"Damn these blinds are dusty. Lucky nobody here has asthma. And there's a dead bee. Wow."

11.03am

"Did you see the email from Jodie about the kitchen sponge? She didn't say my name but I know it's directed at me. Fucking bitch needs to get a life."

11.15am

"Why do we buy this brand of pens? I don't have time to do a scribble every time I need to write something. We should have click pens."

11.26pm

"Oh no. My sock has made its way all the way down into my shoe. I'll have to take my shoe off now."

11.30am

"How is it always my job to change the water bottle? I'm not the only person who drinks water around here. Maybe I won't change it. I'll just bring in my own water."

11.38am

"My ears are hot. Do you ever get that? Hot ears?"

11.41am

"Great. There's that bird again. I know it's the same one because of the pitch. We should get one of those plastic owls. Are pigeons scared of owls? Why are any birds scared of owls? They're all birds."

11.55am

"Ahhh. My leg's gone to sleep. It's because my chair height is all wrong. It'll take me a week to get it back to the way I like it."

12.20pm

"I specifically said no avocado. If I was allergic to avocado I'd be dead by now. Or at least on my way to hospital. What's wrong with people?"

12.48pm

"Have you ever noticed how low the ceilings are? It's like being in a cave. They're definitely lower than normal. I'm going to bring in my tape measure tomorrow."

1.05pm

"Why would anyone use this much tape on a box?"

1.17pm

"Ugh. I just burped and tasted avocado. I should have taken that sandwich back and thrown it at the lady who made it."

1.46pm

"Is this a permanent marker? What idiot puts a permanent marker with the whiteboard markers? No, wait... it's coming off. It's just a bit dry."

2.11pm

"Is there any way to change the volume of the beeps on the photocopier? Why do we even need beeps? Could they be any more annoying? Is it in settings?"

2.17pm

"Is it just me or is it stuffy in here? Pity I can't open my window."

2.30pm

"Oh my God. It's only 2.30. I thought it was like 4 o'clock."

2.54pm

"Who keeps putting sticky notes on the whiteboard? The whiteboard isn't for sticky notes. Stick them somewhere else. Anywhere else. That's why they're sticky."

2.56pm

"How stupid is the word 'recommend'? It's impossible to spell."

2.58pm

"What's that smell? Is it the carpet? I think it's the carpet."

3.25pm

"Fantastic. There goes my other sock. I bought an eight-pack of these so I guess that was a waste of twenty dollars."

3.39pm

"There's... eleven finger prints on my computer screen. No, twelve. People need to learn to point without touching."

3.47pm

"Guess it's my turn to change the printer cartridge. It's always my turn actually. Maybe I should just have my business card changed to Printer Cartridge Changer."

4.03pm

"Is that an ant? Great, now we've got ants."

4.10pm

"Who does Jodie think she is? Just give me the can of Raid and shut the fuck up. I don't need a lecture about ants. I know more about ants than she ever will."

4.30pm

"Wow. Look how dirty this phone cover is. I'm never buying a yellow phone cover again. Not a silicon one anyway."

4.48pm

"Where's my bike helmet? It was right here. I'm sick of people touching my stuff. Guess I'll just have to ride home without a helmet and get knocked off my bike and get a head injury. Oh, here it is."

5.00pm

"Seriously, how loud is this light switch?"

Schewel's

Ian stared out the window and sighed. Schewel's had given him a delivery estimate but it was very broad. 'Sometime between noon and five' meant he'd had to take the whole afternoon off work and he was very busy; there were boxes to be lifted and put back down in a different spot. It wasn't work that anyone could do either. Someone with only one arm couldn't do it for example. A young child wouldn't even be able to get their arms around the boxes. Someone that didn't know what a box was, or how to pick things up and put them down in a different spot, would also have difficulty.

He played his banjo while he waited. Then pickled some beans. He was watching *Delta Force 2* from his Chuck Norris collection on VHS when the delivery people finally arrived. "Anywhere is fine," he told them, "As long as it's facing the television."

The sectional had cost two hundred dollars, almost a week's pay, but it was worth every cent. It was a lot nicer than David's living room furniture. David's furniture was rectangular and uncomfortable looking and didn't have cup holders in the armrests.

23andMe

"Mama Mia!" exclaimed Holly, throwing her hands into the air and waving them about, "Whatsa thisa?"

Twelve of Holly's closest friends and family were waiting for her when she arrived home. They'd rearranged the living room furniture and were seated in a circle. David wasn't happy about this. There was a reason the furniture had been where it was; he'd put a lot of thought into it. He understood this was how some people lived, with chairs plonked close to each other, usually facing the television, but if he wanted to live like trailer trash he would have bought a sectional with cup holders in the armrests from Schewel's. This wasn't about him though. He kept telling himself that. He could move it all back afterwards.

"It's an intervention, Holly. You need help."
"Portobello! I donta needa help, I justa needa spaghetti!"
"You've eaten spaghetti every night for the last two weeks and portobello isn't an exclamation of surprise, it's a mushroom. You have to stop this, Holly. You're not Italian."
"Polenta! The 23andMe results show Ima 3% Italian and 2% Scandinavian. Itsa why I tan easily and like Volvos."

Quick Bedtime Stories for Children Who Don't Deserve One

The Three Bears

Once upon a time there were three bears. Their names were Henry, Roger and Stuart.

The Frog Prince

Once upon a time there was a frog. A green one.

The Princess & the Peas

Once upon a time there was a princess who ate all her peas and grew up strong and healthy.

Winnie the Pooh

"Oh, bother," said Pooh. He was a bear but he could talk and he said that a lot.

Rumpelstiltskin

Once upon a time there was a really short man named Rumpelstiltskin. He was probably German or Russian.

Fridge

Don't ever stick your arms behind the fridge.

A Stone in a Teacup

"Jodie is such a bitch."

"Why, Walter, what did you do?"

"Why do you assume I did something?"

"Because you only ever call Jodie a bitch when she tells you off about something. What did you do?"

"Nothing. That's my point. She's just putting a stone in a teacup."

"Sorry?"

"Who cares if you rinse and squeeze out a sponge after you use it or not? You rinse and squeeze it out before you use it anyway."

"The phrase is 'a *storm* in a teacup', Walter."

"No it isn't. That's stupid. Why would there be a storm in a teacup?"

"It's an idiom meaning a small event that has been exaggerated out of proportion. Why would anyone put a stone in a teacup? It doesn't make any sense."

"It makes a lot more sense than a storm in a teacup. Cups don't have wind or clouds but anyone can drop a stone in one."

"Granted, but why would they?"

"Say you've got a cup of tea that's full to the top."

"Okay."

"Everything's fine and you're about to enjoy your cup of tea and then someone puts a stone in it and it overflows."

"Because you didn't rinse out a sponge?"

"Exactly."

"So your take on the phrase is vengeful displacement?"

"It doesn't matter where it's placed, if the cup is full and you add a stone, it's going to spill everywhere. People like Jodie who put stones in teacups are creating issues for no reason. She's not the boss of the kitchen. She's not the boss of anything. She needs to get out of her high house."

Wow, He Was a Bit Grumpy

It was the first time I'd ever flown first class. My publisher at the time, Penguin, paid for my flight from Washington D.C. to New York to meet and sign contracts. I wouldn't have flown first class otherwise. Usually Holly books my flights which means the cheapest seats on the cheapest airline, with three or four stopovers. If there were a way of putting me with the bags or livestock, she'd find it. Once, to save $340 on the cost of a flight from Australia to the United States, I had stopovers in Burma, Azerbaijan, and Algeria. I'd never even heard of Azerbaijan before the trip. During the flight between Burma and Azerbaijan, the plane shuddered and dipped a lot and I was convinced this was due to the pilot dodging anti-aircraft missiles.

Domestic first class isn't anything like first class on International flights. The seats are a bit more comfy, but that's about it. The first class seats on International flights look like cryogenic pods. Still, I was stoked to be in first class even if it was just domestic; I got to board before everyone else and avoid eye contact with the poor people as they made their way towards the poor people seats at the back of the plane. No damp warm towel for them.

I'm not a huge fan of flying. I'm not frightened that the plane will crash or anything like that, I just see the plane as a flying bus and I'm not a fan of buses. I saw an old magazine advertisement for Pan Am once that showed a couple being served a meal. The dapper couple were sitting in what looked like Lazy-Boy reclining armchairs, and the person serving them was wearing a chef's hat and carving a turkey. The last time I ate on a plane, I had a cube of what I suspect may have been Soylent Green and I had to turn my head sideways to eat it, as the head of the passenger in front of me was less than an inch away from my chin. There may have been something glamorous about flying in the sixties but it's all been downhill since then.

"Good news, we worked out that if we move all the seats fifteen inches closer to the seats in front of them, we can add ten more seats. Cha-ching!"

"That's great but will there be room for people's legs?"

"Some people. Children and midgets mainly."

"Children and midgets?"

"And amputees if they have those skinny metal legs."

"We can't move *all* the seats. The FDA states there has to be a certain amount of clearance in the exit row to meet safety regulations."

"That's not an issue, we'll just charge extra for the additional leg-room in exit row seats. Cha-ching!"

"Well, it's a bit of a cunt move but you had me at the first cha-ching."

Holly and I have a ritual when we fly places; I complain about everything and then we have an argument. Once we land and get to the hotel, I'll declare the hotel is a shithole and that I hate whatever country or city we are in and wished we had gone to Japan instead so I could see the giant robots. After that, I get badly sunburnt. By the third or fourth day I'm fine and we go out shopping for a fridge magnet. Then we leave the next day on a 3AM flight.

Holly wasn't travelling with me to New York so I sent her a photo of my seat with a sadface emoji and the message, "I thought it was going to be like a cryogenic pod. Got a damp warm towel though. It smelled like the moist towelettes you used to get at Kentucky Fried Chicken."

The left side of the plane, where I was seated, had only one seat per row. On the right, the seats were two abreast but there was no one seated beside the man who sat across the aisle from me. The man looked somewhere in his late fifties, well dressed and slim, with short grey hair. He was reading *The New York Times* so I figured he was some kind of businessman, heading to New York to do some business. He'd glanced my way when we first boarded and I'd nodded and smiled as if to say, "Hello fellow first class passenger," but he didn't respond. He also didn't put his luggage in the overhead compartment, just left it in the aisle and sat down, which I found slightly odd.

One of the flying bus waitresses asked the man if he'd like her to stow his luggage and he nodded dismissively without a word. I pegged him as a dickhead, sat back, and flicked through the in-flight magazine. There was an article about glassblowing that was kind of interesting. It's a short flight from D.C. to New York, only an hour and ten minutes, so there was no point watching a movie and I'd forgotten to pack my earphones anyway.

Around fifteen minutes into the flight, a flying bus waitress asked if I'd like a coffee or tea. She was in her late thirties, a little plump, with her blonde hair tied back in a ponytail. I ordered a tea, as did the man sitting across the aisle from me. After she'd poured our drinks and passed them to us, she picked up a blue hardcover notepad and said to the man, "I'm sorry, I don't mean to bother you, but would you mind autographing my book?"

"Why?" asked the man in an Irish accent, "So you can sell it on eBay?"

"Um, no," stammered the flying bus waitress, "It's for me."

"Fine, give it here then. Do you have a pen or do I have to use my own? Oh you do? Well done... Kathy with a K. Can I get back to my newspaper now or would you like a photo as well?"

"Um, that's okay... unless you wouldn't mind."

"I was being sarcastic."

"No," I interrupted, "You were being a dickhead."

I'm not usually one to stand up to unrighteousness. I've been punched before and it's something I'd rather avoid. I wish I was the type of person to leap over embankments and sweep endangered turtles to safety, but some of those punches have been to the face. I haven't had my mettle truly tested of course, and I'd like to think I'd stand up to a true unrighteousness, say if Holly or Seb were attacked, but there's a chance I'd be that guy who pushes everyone aside in their effort to get away. I threw Seb at an angry chicken once.

My highest tested level of 'defending those in need' is when people are rude to the cashier in supermarket checkout lines. I won't say anything to the person being rude, but after they've left I might raise my eyebrows and say to the cashier, "Wow, he was a bit grumpy."

There's no superhero costume for that. Nobody in peril is calling out, "Please help us, Wow He Was a Bit Grumpy Man!"

Sometimes I'm the rude customer. Usually only in McDonald's drive-thrus though. The moment I order anything in an Australian accent at an American McDonald's, the employees roll around on the ground and twitch. There's one particular woman at our local McDonald's who has asked me if I speak English on six separate occasions. Every time I order an Egg McMuffin, she tells me, "I'm sorry, we don't sell burritos."

"I beg your pardon?" said the man, "Are you speaking to me?"

"No, I was talking to the monkey on your shoulder, dickhead."

"It's fine, really," said Kathy the flying bus waitress. She turned to the man, "I'm very sorry, I didn't mean to disturb you."

The man, now glaring at me, dismissed Kathy with a wave. She made her way back towards the cockpit, pulling the drinks cart with her.

"Do you know who I am?" the man asked.

"Yes," I replied, turning my attention back to my magazine, "A dickhead." I was curious at that point but I wasn't going to let him know that.

"This is the last time I'm ever letting a junior assistant organize my itinerary," the man declared, shaking his newspaper and holding it up to read, "I'm surrounded by dim-witted yokels. Australian dim-witted yokels at that apparently."

"Goodo, dickhead."

"Say it once more."

"Dickhead."

"Right."

The man tapped his call button several times. Then several times more. A different flying bus waitress, an older one, walked quickly down the aisle, bent down, and asked if she could help him with something.

"Yes," the man pointed at me, "this Australian is being aggressive towards me and I request that he be moved immediately."

"I'm sorry sir," she responded calmly, "It's a full flight so there's nothing I can do. Unless you'd like to swap with someone in economy class."

"Is that meant to be a joke?" the man asked, "Are you being smart with me?"

"No sir, is there anything else I can help you with?"

"Apparently not. I'll be making a complaint about this and rest assured, I'll never fly this airline again."

"Good."

The man pursed his lips and shook his head but went back to reading his newspaper. His face stayed red for a while and he turned the first few pages loudly, but it was the end of our interaction. I went back to reading my article on glassblowing, finished it, flicked through a few pages of advertisements for expensive watches and luxurious hotels, and stopped...

On the left hand page was a large photo of the man sitting across the aisle from me. His hair was a bit longer in the photo and he was wearing a huge scarf, but it was unmistakably him. I felt like I was experiencing some kind of reality glitch. The right hand page of the article was titled, *Method of Madness: Behind the many roles of Daniel Day-Lewis.*

The article, featuring three or four photos of Daniel being contemplative and one of him laughing at something hilarious, maybe one of his own jokes, was basically a run-down of Daniel Day-Lewis's acting methods. Apparently he takes himself pretty seriously and is a 'method actor' which means staying in character even when off set or something. I could probably Google method acting but then I'll get ads for face paint and wigs for several weeks. I dedicate one day a week, Bird Thursday, to Googling birdseed, birdhouses, and birdbaths. This way all of my ads feature pictures of birds instead of butt plugs and Hatsune Miku body pillows.

According to the article, during the filming of *My Left Foot*, Daniel Day-Lewis stayed in character for his portrayal of a wheelchair-bound person with Cerebral Palsy for the entire shooting schedule. This meant crew members had to feed him and carry him over cables, to and from set in a wheelchair, and help him use the bathroom for two or three months. If I were one of the crewmembers and my boss said, "David, I'm going to need you to wipe Daniel's arse because he's pretending he can't do it himself," I would have resigned immediately. On the way out, I would have mentioned to Daniel Day-Lewis that Robert Downey Jr. makes forty times what he does for superhero movies.

I haven't seen *My Left Foot*, because I don't watch movies about feet, but from what I can tell it's about a guy in a wheelchair who can move his left foot. I can move both my feet and nobody has approached me about the movie rights.

"So, David, we received your script titled *My Left and Right Foot and My Legs and Both My Arms and Hands*, but we're a little confused by the plot. It's about a man who has full working use of all his limbs?"

"That's right. He's perfectly fine."

"Okay. Does he have any special abilities or talents?"

"No, not really. He can draw a little bit."

"Oh, portraits and the like?"

"No, just cats."

I haven't actually seen *any* of Daniel's movies, so I can't comment on his acting ability, but I know him as the type of person that says, "Do you know who I am?" and probably, "Do you like my outfit? It's a wheat sack. Because I play a wheat sack in my next movie. A seventeenth-century wheat sack with Parkinson's disease. I expect I'll get another Golden Globe award. Where to put it? Hahaha. We should go to my house and watch all of my movies. I have a home theatre. It's called The Daniel-Day Lewis theatre. I'm going to need you to carry me there on your shoulders."

For those who haven't read *Method of Madness: Behind the many roles of Daniel Day-Lewis* and those, like myself, who haven't seen any of his award-winning performances, here's a quick breakdown of some of Daniel's better known movies, and the preparation he took to play each role:

There Will Be Blood

Daniel Day-Lewis plays a dentist who is terrible at putting his patients at ease. To prepare for this role, Daniel spent a year living inside his own mouth as a tooth.

The Boxer

Daniel Day-Lewis plays a dog. To prepare for this role, he developed early degenerative hip dysplasia and had to be put down.

My left Foot

Daniel Day-Lewis plays a left foot. To prepare for this role, he spent twelve months in a giant sock.

Lincoln

Daniel Day-Lewis plays an automobile. To prepare for this role, he was owned for thirty years by an old man who kept his Tommy Bahama hat on Daniel's rear window shelf.

Phantom Thread

Daniel Day-Lewis plays a six-inch strand of cotton. To prepare for this role, Daniel built his own podracer and competed in the Boonta Eve Classic. Yes, they're getting worse but *Star Wars* fans might appreciate the effort. I had a mental glitch and couldn't remember the term 'podracer' so I Googled 'Thing little Darth Vader drives' and now I'm getting adverts for *Star Wars* Lego. I bought a Millennium Falcon which I'll have to hide it in the closet because Holly and I recently had a discussion about unnecessary Amazon purchases. She has no appreciation for art and made me send back a levitating moon lamp.

Gangs of New York

Daniel Day-Lewis plays a switchblade. To prepare for this role, Daniel spent a year jumping really quickly out of boxes. I did state that they were getting worse. I wouldn't even bother with the last one, it's just a dig at hairdressers. I know a guy named Chaz who just completed a hairdressing course and he's acting like he gained his PHD in astrophysics.

The Last of the Mohicans

Daniel Day-Lewis plays a haircut. To prepare for this role, Daniel took a three-week community college course to become a fully qualified hairdresser.

5 Hours, 16 Minutes

It hurt. Everywhere. There were bugs crawling under his skin. He pulled back sweat-soaked sleeves and scratched his forearms vigorously, scratched his neck, his face. Even his hair hurt and he banged his fists against the side of his head and yelled in frustration.

It had been five hours and sixteen minutes since his last fix - the longest he'd gone in three years. He'd promised himself that it was the last time, promised others, and he'd meant it at the time. This wasn't who he wanted to be. Want isn't as strong as need though.

"Just once more," he pleaded.

"You can do this," Lori whispered, squeezing his hand, "*We* can do this. Together."

"I thought I could but I can't, it's too hard. You don't understand what it's like. Just once more then never again. I swear."

"Alright," Lori sighed sadly, "Once more and then it has to end. One way or another."

"Thank you," sobbed JM with relief. He scrolled quickly through Facebook memes about Democrats, stopped on one, chuckled, and clicked the share button.

Pizza Meme

My friend JM shared a meme on his Facebook page about ordering pizza today. It's not unusual for JM to share memes - he does so fifteen or twenty times per day - but they're usually about transgender Mexicans having abortions or the right to arm yourself against Hillary's deleted emails.

One might assume he shares these memes to spark healthy political conversation, but one would be wrong. He shares them because people go up to him afterwards and thank him for sharing them. Hundreds of people apparently. They cheer and shake his hand and slap him on the back and then there's a parade in his honor.

"Guns don't kill people, people kill people."
"Holy shit that's clever, JM. It certainly puts those Liberals in their place. The NRA should use that as their slogan. I showed it to the lads here and we've all decided to get t-shirts made up with it on it and we're hiring a bus so that we can all come around to your house and shake your hand personally - maybe get a few photos taken with you. Also, we did a bit of a whip-around to get you a present. It's nothing major, just a week at a Sandal's resort, but apparently they have a water slide that goes through an aquarium."

"That wasn't necessary, Cletus; but thank you. I'm just happy to provide food for thought. If you liked that one, you might also like my 'Mowers don't mow lawns, people mow lawns.' meme. Or my one about grills and sausages."

"Would the mower one work with weed-whackers?"

'Well sure."

"That's genius. Stupid fucking Liberals."

It's true of course, guns don't kill people. The guns would be perfectly safe if people left them alone. The NRA has always said this, and they've always been correct, but somehow they don't understand the implications of what they're saying and have avoided their own conclusion. The fact that such a slogan is so evidently contradictory to the interests of a Gun Club says a lot about the institution and its place in the political process, but hey, it doesn't contain words over two syllables and fits on a bumper sticker.

Usually when JM shares a stupid meme, I make a sarcastic comment and he sends me a fourteen-paragraph angry message and doesn't talk to me for a week. Once, after he shared a meme about 'illegal' Mexican farm workers, I commented with an image of his face Photoshopped onto a head of corn with a speech bubble saying, "They took our cobs!" and he actually unfriended me. He sent me a re-friend request a week later though. I left him hanging for a few days but then he shared a meme about vegetarians at barbecues and I had to accept his friend request to post the comment, "They took our kabobs!"

I might actually copy & paste the last couple of JM's angry texts because it's good to keep a record of these things...

June 12 2019 3.26PM

"I guess you think it's pretty fucking hilarious to stick pictures of my face on things but I'm not laughing. This is the 9th time you've done it and I've had enough. Stay the fuck off my Facebook page if you don't have anything better to do than post stupid shit. You crossed a line and I won't accept anything less than a written apology. This is not ok."

July 18 2019 11.08AM

"You're uninvited from camping this weekend. If you show up, you'll be told to leave. I don't give a fuck if you've already packed and made soup. Nobody likes your soup anyway asshole."

July 18 2019 11.28AM

"I apologize for saying nobody likes your soup. You're still uninvited from deer camp but my comment about your soup was uncalled for."

July 27 2019 4.05PM

"I don't care if you call a cantaloupe a rock melon in Australia, I don't appreciate my face being put on one."

August 4 2019 12.38PM

"One more post and your toast."

That last one rhymed so I replied with my own poem:

Roses are red, JM is blue.
It's you're, not your, and my post was misconstrued.
You're entitled to the views you advocated.
I was calling them, not you, asinine and antiquated.
I'm sorry seeing your face on a bok choy caused you distress.
Please accept my friend request.

Our biggest falling out was when JM posted a meme about soldiers and Jesus, and I suggested truck drivers, teachers, construction workers, and even shop assistants - sacrificing time away from their loved ones to perform a dangerous job that facilitates our way of life - deserved just as many 'thoughts and prayers as soldiers. They cost nothing and have no redeemable value, so why not give them out freely?

"Hello, I'd like to redeem these thoughts and prayers, please."
"Sure, how many do have?"
"Sixteen. My wife is pretty active on Facebook."
"Nice. You can get a Breville toaster for that."

This was, of course, construed as 'kids flipping burgers for minimum wage sacrifice just as much as a member of Seal Team 6', and JM wrote me a three-volume novel about the time he rode in a submarine and how he once saw a shark and how small the bunks were. There may have been something in there about eagles and the love of a good woman as well.

I didn't read it all because I was busy hanging up posters of Lenin and Chairman Mao while plotting to subvert the American dream and turn everyone into potato farmers.

We always make up eventually though. Because we're both semi-functioning adults and, despite our vast differences in political views and good looks, I love JM like a brother. The kind of brother that takes medicine to control his behavioural disorders but will still help you build a tree house. I agree to stop posting pictures of JM's face Photoshopped onto produce, and JM makes an effort to avoid sharing Russian troll farm memes for a few days and only share memes about stopping for school buses and ordering pizza. They're memes that JM feels are too innocuous to attract criticism and/or sarcastic comment. Which makes it more of a challenge.

The pizza meme that JM posted today stated that if you are ever in a violent situation and fear for your life, you should dial the police and order a large pizza. The meme specified pepperoni but I don't think it matters, and it doesn't work the other way; you can't call Pizza Hut and ask for the police. Apparently the savvy emergency dispatcher, who has seen the meme, will know what's up, and send a vehicle to your house. Which might work in a small percentage of violent situations occurring just before dinner, but it's a bit of a stretch. Also, you have to be home for it to work. You can't do it if you are being mugged in an alley or hiking and come across a bear.

David Thorne

Like • Reply • 17m

 JM Didn't we just talk about this?

Like • Reply • 12m

Anne Hathaway

"I'm ordering pizza."

"I've seen the meme, Holly. I know you're calling the police."

"Why would I be calling the police?"

"Because you asked if I think Anne Hathaway is attractive and I said she's not bad."

"She isn't attractive at all. Her face is too big for her head."

"Okay."

"You don't think her face is too big for her head?"

"I hadn't really noticed."

"You love her, don't you?"

"No, I just don't think her face is as big as you're making it out to be."

"Well it is. It's like she's looking into a magnified makeup mirror. But all the time. You really don't think so?"

"If I say I do, can we end this conversation?"

"Yes."

"Fine. From certain angles, her face does look big."

"No, all angles."

"What if you were standing directly behind her?"

"You'd see her face sticking out the sides. Do you want pizza or not?"

"Only if I can watch you dial."

Home Haircuts

A step-by-step guide

So you've decided to cut your own hair. Congratulations. You're embarking on a journey of discovery and savings the whole family can enjoy. Before you begin this journey, you will need to purchase a set of electric clippers. Wal-Mart carries a large range of Wahl brand clippers but I prefer the Oster Classic 76 Professional in orange because I'm not poor.

Cutting your children's hair

Go for it. They're never going to let you cut their hair again, so be creative. This is an excellent opportunity to discover what the different length blade-combs do and learn from your mistakes.

Cutting your own hair

Step 1. State you are only going to 'clean it up a bit'.
Step 2. Cut it way too short.
Step 3. Don't leave the house for two weeks.
Step 4. Swear that you are never going to cut it that short again.
Step 5. Repeat.

Aaaaaron

The branding agency I work for fired a junior graphic designer named Aaaaaron last month. I realize I may have added too many A's to Aaaaaron's name but there were too many to begin with and it's easier to just hold down the A key for a bit than remember the correct number. I assume Aaaaaron's parents wanted him to be first on lists or something but if that was the case, Aardvark would have sufficed.

Mike, our Creative Director, had me break the news to Aaaaaron as Mike avoids confrontation. Once, when an angry client turned up unexpectedly with his lawyer, I watched from my office window as Mike jumped the back fence and ran down an alley. Twelve-thousand brochures for landscaping services had been printed and mailed out with the caption under a photo of guy pruning a hedge stating, "Ben hasn't supplied any text for this yet. Please inform the useless cunt he has 2 days before this goes to print. Also, who ate all the cake in the kitchen? Was it Jodie?"

Aaaaaron wasn't very good at his job and he smelled like a baby. Someone once told me that this is how all Caucasians smell to Asians, because Asians don't drink milk, but I asked my Asian friend Brian if this was true and he replied, "No, we drink milk, dickhead. Who told you that?"

Aaaaaron didn't take the news of his dismissal well. He'd signed a lease on an apartment close to the agency and bought expensive boots the day before.

"You can't fire me. I have a contract."
"Yes, which states in the first paragraph that you're on a three month trial period. You've been here less than two weeks."
"I just rented an apartment. And I bought these boots yesterday. They're Frye."
"Frye make men's boots?"
"Yes."
"Nice. Did you keep the receipt?"
"No."
"Pity, you could have taken them back. Got yourself a pair of Hush Puppies instead."
"You think this a joke? How am I meant to pay my rent?"
"Perhaps you should have thought about that before you lied on your résumé."
"That doesn't make any sense, I wrote my résumé six months ago. And I didn't lie on it."
"It states you're proficient in Illustrator."
"So?"
"You took an hour to draw a circle this morning."
"And colour it."
"Sure. Had you ever used Illustrator before starting here, Aaaaaron?"

"Yes. Well, FreeHand actually. It's a much better program than Illustrator."

"I agree. Freehand is far more intuitive. Unfortunately, its last update was in 2003 and it won't run on computers manufactured after 2011. What about Photoshop?"

"I never said I was proficient at Photoshop."

"No, you said you were 'adept'."

"Adept isn't as good as proficient."

"Taking two days to turn an image to greyscale is hardly adept. A five-year-old could have Googled how to do it in ten minutes. Have you ever used Google?"

"Fuck you."

"Sorry?

Fuck you. I was going to quit anyway. This job sucks and you're all a bunch of pretentious wankers."

"Right, well that works out perfectly for everyone then. We accept your resignation. All the best with your future endeavors and let me know if you need a reference."

"You're going to be seriously fucking sorry."

"I already am, Aaaaaron. Still, live and learn; we'll probably make your replacement do some kind of test to make sure they didn't just Google 'what programs do graphic designers use?' for their resume."

"You'll see."

Aaaaaron kicked the photocopier on his way out of the boardroom. It was a decent kick and dented a panel so we'll have to get that replaced. The kick also left a decent scuff on his right Frye boot, so there's no way he's going to be able to return them and he may have broken a toe because he made a weird surprised face and shook his hands up and down as if he was having a seizure before limping upstairs to collect his stuff.

Graphic designers tend to be melodramatic and I've seen much worse. I myself have been known to 'chuck a fruity' but it's usually more of a internal fruity than an external one; emails are written and rumours are started and dishes in the sink are clinked louder than they need to be, but I don't kick photocopiers or lock my door and sob loud enough for other's to hear so they try to get in to ask me what's wrong so I can yell, "I just want to be left alone!" *

Once, when I worked at an agency called de Masi jones, we went on a three-day staff retreat and Lillian, our senior designer, set fire to a hut and destroyed two kayaks with an axe. She was in love with Thomas, the owner of the agency, and while Thomas was passed out drunk the first night, Lillian went through his phone messages and learned he'd had sex with the Asian lady who cleans his apartment. It was a one-time thing, and had cost Thomas two hundred dollars, but it had happened on the same day that Lillian made him cabbage soup for lunch at work.

---

* *Honestly, Jodie, nobody cares. Sob by all means but do it quietly. You sound like a barn owl with Down syndrome. The only thing worse than hearing your 'Hoo Hoo Hooooo' performance is watching you eat.*

We assumed the photocopier attack was the extent of Aaaaaron's revenge but he returned at 1.17am that night with a brick. We know it was 1.17am because the security video is time stamped. The footage showed Aaaaaron pulling his purple Kia Soul up outside the office, with his number plate clearly visible, and attempting to throw the brick without getting out of his car. The brick made the distance but it mustn't have had much momentum as it bounced off the window. Aaaaaron had to open his car door and get out to retrieve the brick and he put some real effort into his second throw; the glass shattered and the alarm sounded.

I've set the alarm off by accident before and the pitch, volume, and strobe lighting made my legs go wobbly. Aaaaaron obviously hadn't anticipated the alarm as he made the same face and hand thing he'd done when he kicked the photocopier, then ran off - apparently completely forgetting that he'd driven. He returned a few minutes later, sprinting into view, and practically dived into his car - striking his head on the doorframe as he did so.

There was no sound in the footage but it must have made a decent 'dong'. Possibly stunned by the blow, Aaaaaron put his car into reverse, with the door still open, and slammed the accelerator. The door hit a No Parking sign and bent backwards - it must have damaged the hinges because Aaaaaron had to get out and kick it to get it closed. He couldn't open it again so he ran around to the passenger side and climbed through before driving off.

Mike and I watched the video footage in his office the next morning. We chuckled when the brick bounced off the window but were in tears by the time Aaaaaron made his getaway. Other staff members made their way in to see what the howls were about and we rewatched the footage probably thirty times. Somehow it became funnier with each viewing and at one point Mike had to lie on the floor because he couldn't breathe.

We'd initially intended to notify the police but collectively agreed that the entertainment was worth the inconvenience of having the window replaced. And that Aaaaaron obviously had enough issues to deal with without being arrested. Besides, he wasn't wrong; we are all pretentious wankers and working here really does suck. It probably sucks less than being homeless and unemployed with a broken toe and concussion and having to climb across the passenger seat to get into a Kia Soul though.

I saw Aaaaaron in a supermarket a week or so later. He was buying bananas and pancake mix and had a large purple bruise with stitches on his forehead. I was a few people behind him in the checkout queue, but he saw me. He pretended he hadn't but his face went red and sweaty and the checkout girl asked him if he was okay. He said he was so that's good. His card was declined though.

The Attic

The first few nights, before she'd thought to cover the insulation batts with blankets, she'd woken several times during the night. It was itchy and uncomfortable and she'd developed a rash. It was surprisingly comfortable now. She'd added a pillow and created a small shelf between two trusses on which she kept a flashlight, snacks, drinking water, and a bottle to pee in.

She had to be quiet - if they heard her moving around they might think there were possums in the attic and investigate - but it was an old house and the inherent creaks disguised any small noises she inadvertently made.

She positioned her eye over the small hole she'd drilled above Seb's bed and peered down. Below, Seb was snoring softly. The RGB lights in the gaming machine he'd built illuminated the room just enough for her to make out his jawline. His lips. His tussled hair. Seb muttered something in his sleep and rolled over. She smiled, wondering what he was dreaming about.

"Goodnight my love," Rebekah whispered, "I'll see you in the morning. Through the bathroom hole."

Slovenian Models

"Okay, Melania, do you understand what we are we going to be doing today?"

"You are going to take photos of me."

"Yes, I am going to take photos of you without your clothes on."

"Okay."

"Holding an orange."

"A real orange?"

"Yes."

"Do I get to keep the orange?"

"That depends on how well the photo-shoot goes."

"Okay."

Four-Hour Showers

People often ask me why I moved from Australia to live in Virginia in the United States. By often, I mean every six months or so. It depends if I've been social or not. Sometimes I don't leave the house for several months so I'm not asked anything during that time except, "Are you alive?" Usually by text-message because I rarely answer my phone in case it's someone asking if I want to go out. I don't have agoraphobia or debilitating social anxiety, I'm just basically lazy. Even the thought of getting ready to go somewhere tires me out; "Which shoes do I wear with these pants? Do I have clean socks? When did I last shave my ears?" It's all too much.

I tell people I moved for love, or work, or because Virginia has squirrels and snow, but the truth is, I moved for the cigarettes. They're around five dollars a pack in Virginia. In Australia, a pack of cigarettes is around thirty-five dollars. That's not a typo and the difference between the Australian and US dollar value is negligible. It's meant to make it difficult for teenagers to take up smoking, and I'm sure there are supporting statistics, but it's also resulted in low-income established smokers choosing nicotine over food for their kids. Which is completely understandable.

"I'm hungry, what's for dinner?"

"Second-hand smoke."

"We had that last night."

"Blame the government. And drink your Coke."

"That's not coke. It's just a glass of tap water with Coke written on the side with a Sharpie."

"Less complaining and more deep inhalation please."

My friend Ross visited from Australia recently. It was meant to be a five-day holiday but he lost his job just before flying out and announced, in the car after Holly and I picked him up from Dulles Airport, "Good news; I can stay five or six weeks."

I first met Ross nearly thirty years ago in a record store. I was waiting in line, holding a copy of *Phantasmagoria* by The Damned, and Ross, standing in line behind me, stated, "Excellent choice. I really like track four, *Sanctum Sanctorum*. If you close your eyes while you listen to it, it's like you're standing in the ruins of a church at night. Like in England somewhere. Or maybe Bulgaria. Do you want to buy some weed?"

We started hanging out after that and spent most of our weekends standing around in the middle of our local mall discussing bats and being misunderstood. We weren't full-blown Goths but we owned belts with studs in them and had the right hair. Ross even got his tongue pierced before it became commonplace. It became infected and now he can't taste watermelon. I considered getting my eyebrow pierced at the same time but I read somewhere that it can cause partial face paralysis so I decided not to. My uncle Keith had paralysis on left side of his face, from a stroke, and it wasn't pleasant to look at. The half that wasn't paralyzed was pretty dreadful to look at too though, so it's not as if his stroke meant the loss of any potential modeling contracts. If anything, the paralyzed side looked better; like it was just hanging out relaxed, maybe sleeping. To make up for the loss of expression, Keith over-emphasized his 'good side' expressions like a coked-up ventriloquist dummy. Slight smiles were terrifying grins, a raised eyebrow looked like he was riding in one of those spinning things that astronauts train in, and a mildly cross look looked like he was straining to push out the world's largest poo. Sometimes I'd hold up my hand so I could only see the paralyzed side of his face while he was talking to me. He didn't like that much and would take his poo straining expression to new levels. He had a second stroke a few years after the first, which balanced things out a bit, but his third stroke killed him. He died in an airplane toilet during a flight from Adelaide to Sydney, which is only worth mentioning as it supports my early statement about making sure your hair looks nice and deleting your browser history before taking a dump.

Ross and I eventually grew out of our Goth phase and Ross moved to Sydney to work as sales rep for a cardboard box company. We caught up every so often but this was the first time we'd seen each other since I'd moved to America.

There's a saying about fish and houseguests smelling after three days but Ross took four-hour showers, two or three times a day, so smell wasn't as much of an issue as clogged drains.* I enjoy a long shower myself but I don't think I've ever had one that lasted more than thirty minutes - most of the showers I took while Ross was staying with us were less than three seconds as there was never any hot water. I don't do the polar bear club thing. At one point, after heating a bowl of water in the microwave and washing myself with a flannel, I questioned why Ross spent so much time in the shower and he explained he liked to drink a couple of beers and watch Netflix movies on his iPad in there.

"But you were in there for four hours this morning."
"That's not my fault. I didn't tell Peter Jackson to make *The Lord of the Rings* so long. Plus I have to leave my hair conditioner in for five minutes."

I'm not exactly sure how Ross lost his job, his version depended on how much he'd had to drink, but apparently the Human Resources Manager - a large woman named Carol - had it out for Ross from day one and, "Really, they should need a warrant to check your desk drawers."

"So what are you going to do?"
"Order another round of beers and then sing karaoke."
"No, I meant about employment."

---

* *Ross is very hairy.*

"I'll work something out. I hated that job anyway. I was a like a clipped kingfisher."

"Sorry?"

"A kingfisher with it's wings clipped. So it can't fly away."

"Why a kingfisher?"

"What's wrong with kingfishers?"

"Nothing, but the type of bird isn't generally specified in the analogy about clipped wings. It's just a bit strange that you chose a Kingfisher."

"They dive into the water to catch fish."

"So?"

"Name one other bird that dives into the water to catch fish."

"Pelicans."

"Do they? Regardless, nobody keeps pelicans as pets."

"Do people keep kingfishers as pets?"

"That's not the point. If I were a bird, I'd be a Kingfisher. It's my favourite bird. What's yours?"

"I don't know, maybe the African Grey Parrot."

"Weak. Parrots can't dive for fish."

"Parrots can speak. I'll just ask you for a fish."

"I'm not giving you any of my fish. Ask Holly what her favourite bird is."

"Holly, what's your favourite bird?"

"What? Why?"

"So Ross can tell you it's weak because it can't dive for fish."

"I quite like cardinals. It's the state bird of Virginia."

"What did she say?"

"She said she likes cardinals."

"Weak."

177

Ross received a decent redundancy cheque but blew through most of it while he was in America. Mainly due to his ability to go into any bar and leave with drugs a few minutes later. I'm not sure if it's an innate gift or developed through years of experience, but Ross has the drug version of 'gaydar' and can spot someone who will sell him drugs, or knows someone who will sell him drugs, within seconds of walking into any bar.

"But how do you know you're not approaching an off duty police officer?"

"I can tell by the jacket they're wearing."

"Really?"

"Yes, see I'd be able to tell you're not a police officer if I didn't know you, because you're wearing a Superdry jacket. Police officers don't shop at Superdry. They shop at department stores like J.C. Penny's."

"So the trick is to only approach people wearing brand name jackets?"

"Certain brand names. The expensive ones. I wouldn't approach anyone wearing a Columbia jacket for example. Police officers like Columbia jackets. And brown leather jackets with a strap thing instead of a collar."

"What are you going to do if they catch on to your strategy and start issuing officers G-Star and Diesel jackets?

"I can tell by the pants as well."

"It's just sheer luck you haven't approached a police officer yet, isn't it?"

"Yes, probably."

I don't recall much of Ross's five or six week visit, as we visited a lot of bars, but I have photos of us on top of the Empire State Building, standing in front of the White House gates, standing in a cave, shooting shotguns in a quarry, Salsa dancing, jumping on a hotel mattress, and riding a really big pig in a paddock. We actually got into trouble for riding the pig. The farmer blocked my car with his tractor to stop us leaving and threatened to call the sheriff. Ross had drugs on him so it was in our best interests to offer the farmer some form of compensation.

"I was thinking more along the lines of fifty dollars. Three hundred dollars for riding your pig is outrageous."

"Fine, I'll call the sheriff and we'll let him deal with it. We don't take kindly to trespassers around here."

"It's not as if we were rustling cattle or poisoning your well. We were only on the pig for about ten seconds and he looked like he was having fun."

"She."

"Sorry?"

"Tammy."

"The pig's name is Tammy?"

"You have a problem with that?"

"No, I have a problem with paying three hundred dollars for ten seconds on Tammy. We said we were sorry."

"You were trespassing. You're lucky I didn't shoot you. Three hundred dollars or I'm calling the sheriff."

"One hundred dollars and we get to ride Tammy again."

"Deal."

The morning of his flight back to Australia, Ross worked out how he was going to do to make a living when he got home; he had a small bit of money left over after his vacation and decided to invest it in a foolproof venture.

"Invest it in what?"

"Cigarettes. Thirty cartons of cigarettes."

"You don't smoke."

"I'm not going to smoke the cigarettes, I'm going to sell them. A single pack of cigarettes in Australia costs thirty-five dollars. If I buy the packs here for five dollars each and sell them there for twenty five, that's a twenty dollar profit per pack. Thirty cartons of cigarettes contain three hundred packs and twenty bucks times three hundred comes to six grand. And, there's nothing to stop me coming back in a month and doing it all over again."

"You'll be a jet-setting International tobacco entrepreneur."

"Exactly."

"So you're just going to walk into bars in Australia and yell, 'Cigarettes for sale, get your cigarettes here!'? Are you going to use a little wooden tray with a strap that goes around your neck to display them on?"

"No, I'll put them in my backpack. And I'm not going to yell anything as I'm only going to sell the cigarettes to mates. I know dozens of people who smoke and will jump at the chance to save ten dollars a pack."

"Did you check the Australian Customs website to check if there's a limit on how many cigarettes can be taken into the country?"

"Of course I did."

"Well you certainly seem to have it all thought out, Ross. How long have you been planning this?"

"For the last four hours. While I was in the shower."

"I wanted to mention that actually. We received our water bill and it's four thousand dollars higher than normal."

"Really? You should ask them to check the meter. You might have a leak."

We had to drive to four different stores to buy the thirty cartons of Marlboro Lights, and to TJ Maxx to buy a suitcase to transport them all in. It cost Ross fifteen hundred dollars for the cigarettes - and another fifty dollars for the Juicy Couture suitcase - but he was pretty sure he could claim the costs as business expenses.

"Oh, and I have something for you and Holly to say thanks for letting me stay."

"That wasn't necessary, Ross."

"Here you go."

"A carton of cigarettes? You shouldn't have."

"That's the brand you smoke isn't it?"

"No, but it's the thought that counts."

"Oh right, I might keep them then. That carton is worth a lot of money in Australia."

Ross hadn't checked the Australian customs website to see if there's a limit on how many cigarettes can be taken into the country.

Customs officers confiscated all but two packs when Ross landed in Sydney and he had to pay a fine. They gave him the option of paying a ninety-cent tax on each cigarette to keep them, but he'd invested the last of his redundancy cheque on the venture and didn't have another six grand. He might have avoided the fine but when asked what was in the Juicy Couture suitcase, Ross stated, "Souvenirs… fridge magnets and stuff," and, when they actually checked, added, "Oh, and some cigarettes. I forgot about those."

Ross had to move back in with his parents last week. He's not happy about this as it's an old house with a small water heater and his father limits his showers to six minutes. He uses a kitchen timer and turns the water off at the mains if Ross is a second over. It was originally five minutes but Ross successfully negotiated additional time by showing his dad the hair conditioner bottle label.

Seven Seconds

While having lunch at work today, my coworker Ben stated, "If a fly lands on your food, you have to count to seven before shooing it away."

His logic behind this is apparently based on how flies eat: When a fly lands on food, it vomits on it, waits for the vomit to dissolve the food, then sucks the vomit and the dissolved food back up with some kind of straw thing on its face. Shooing away the fly before it sucks back up the vomit and dissolved food means you eat the fly's vomit.

"So you just let flies sit on your food?"
"For seven seconds, yes."
"Do you use a timer or count in your head?"
"I use the hippopotamus method. One hippopotamus, two hippopotamus etcetera. It's more exact than the Mississippi method. When you say Mississippi, it's easy to run the syllables together. You can't do that with hippopotamus."
"Sure. Technically it would be 'one hippopotamus, two hippopotamuses though. That's an extra syllable."
"I'm not counting hippopotamuses, I'm just using the word hippopotamus between the numbers as a timer. Besides, if I were counting hippopotamuses, I'd use hippopotami which

has the same amount of syllables."

"Do you continue eating while you count or wait patiently for the fly to finish?"

"It depends on the food. If it's a proper dinner and a fly lands on the mashed potatoes, I'll eat some carrots or peas while it finishes. If it's a sandwich, obviously I'd have to wait the full seven seconds."

"That's assuming all flies take exactly seven seconds to eat. You might get a particularly ravenous one who finishes in six seconds. Which could mean eating a second round of vomit."

"No, they all take exactly seven seconds. They have a built-in clock. Like cicadas."

Dating Websites

We all tell lies. Especially when we're young. When I was in fifth grade, I told everyone at school my father was a motorcycle stuntman. I'm not sure why. I'd watched a television documentary about Evel Knievel around that time, so maybe that had something to do with it. My best friend at the time, Matthew, didn't back me up at all.

"Your dad works at the post office with my dad."
"Yes, Matthew, he hurt his leg in a crash so he's having a short break from stunt riding. When his leg is better, he's going to jump fifty buses to break the world record."
"You've never said anything about this before."
"That's because it's meant to be a secret. The bus companies don't like people jumping their buses. If you crash, it dents the roof."
"Your dad doesn't even have a motorcycle."
"Yes he does, Matthew, a Super Honda 5000 jet bike. It's in the shed. That's why you haven't seen it."
"Can I come over and see it then?"
"Um, yes."
"After school today?"
"No, I can't today. I have ninja practice."

Most of us grow out of the need to fabricate stories to impress others. The outright lies become embellishments and everyone expects some degree of embellishment in stories. A bear you once saw might be described as bigger and closer, the four beers you drank at a party becomes ten to justify kissing a fat girl named Susan, and a six-inch garden snake you once flicked off the patio furniture with a stick becomes a village menace responsible for taking livestock.

"You flicked it off?"

"Yes."

"With your hand?"

"No, I used a stick. It was pretty short stick though."

"What kind of snake was it?"

"I'm not sure. I'm not an expert on snakes. Probably some kind of anaconda."

"Really? How big was it?"

"It was coiled so it was hard to tell. Probably six feet. Maybe seven stretched out."

"Damn. You're lucky you weren't bitten."

"Yes, it lunged at me but I narrowly avoided its four-inch fangs by performing a backwards flip."

"Wow, where did you learn to do a backwards flip?"

"Ninja practice."

Some people never grow out of the need to construct outright lies. The lies make them bigger. Better. More interesting. Sometimes it's all they have. All they are.

Thomas, the creative director of a branding agency I used to work for, once told me he had sex with three girls at the same time. Two of them were apparently twins, named Ashley and Kate, and the third was a gymnast named Laura. I knew the story wasn't true but I hadn't known Thomas for very long at that point, so I nodded and feigned astonishment at his sexual prowess.

"Gosh. How did you keep up with them?"
"I have a lot of stamina. I work out and take supplements. Plus I run 10K each morning and play tennis. I'm in division one."
"Very impressive. Twins you said?"
"Yes, they weren't identical twins but they both had blonde hair."
"That's plausible. What colour was Laura's hair?"
"Black. She wore it in pigtails like that chick on *NCIS*."
"The edgy computer whiz?"
"Yes, but Laura was way hotter. She looked a lot like Anne Hathaway."
"Nice. And you said she was a gymnast?"
"Yes, well a trapeze artist actually. For Cirque du Soleil. Also, I have cancer."

Thomas told me the same story several months later, but the trapeze artist became a divorced Philharmonic Orchestra violinist named Jessica, who was into anal play, and the twins, Jasmine and Tory, were her stepdaughters. Also, Thomas was their tennis coach.

Alternative truths were a recurring theme with Thomas. It's possible he did sleep with twins and their talented mother, but the likelihood of a gothic Anne Hathaway saying to her twin blonde stepdaughters, "Let's fuck that middle-aged fat guy wearing skinny jeans, I'll grab my anal beads!" seems pretty slim. If he'd instead made it 'a stay-at-home mother and her two mentally handicapped adult daughters' it might have passed as vaguely plausible, but there'd need to be some kind of backstory. Like he'd been a family friend for years and the daughters only had six months to live and they didn't want to die virgins or something. And maybe lose the part where they all tongue-kiss.

I won't go into all the embellished realities Thomas told during the seven years I worked with him, as this book would be volume one of a thirty volume set, but they included: Having a photographic memory and being able to read novels in under a minute; having cancer and only two years to live; being a fully qualified 747 pilot; being related to Robin Hood; dating Nicole Kidman; owning nude photos of Nicole Kidman; having lived in Japan for several years; being able to hold his breath for seven minutes; having donated a kidney; having a small role in the movie *Gallipoli*; having sex with Brooke Satchwell from *Neighbours* in a yurt; owning a catamaran; and having a twelve inch penis. I saw his penis when he was drunk one night and it looked like a baby turtle's head peeking out of a hairy shell.

If there was one place where Thomas could truly let his creativity soar, it was on online dating websites. He was a member of approximately twenty dating sites such a Match, Zoosk, and Adult Friend Finder. I've no doubt he has a Tinder account these days, with a profile stating he's an FBI astronaut and four-time Wimbledon champion, but Tinder hadn't been invented back then.

Thomas went to a meeting one afternoon, with several dating site windows left open behind his email, and I discovered his dating accounts while looking for a file. I get that it's an outrageous invasion of privacy, but some of the statements Thomas made to the girls online were too incredulous not to screenshot and email to myself. Those screenshots have been floating about in my 'qwtefqwtyer' image folder for a few years but I thought I'd copy a few down *verbatim* for posterity. Be forewarned, some of these may make you feel queasy:

Adult Friend Finder

"Yeah, been living on my yacht for nearly three years now. When it came time to buy property I thought do I want to live in a penthouse apartment or at a mariner with ever changing views? So yeah, it's not a big yacht just two bedrooms but it's more than big enough for me and my cat Brody. Maybe someday I'll want the white picket fence but for now I'm happy. There's nothing quite like drifting off to sleep rocked by the waves. Hopefully you'll get to experience it soon cutie. Heehee. ;)"

Match

"Sorry I didn't get back to you sooner babe. Super busy weekend. I had to do catwalk for my fashion designer friend Brody. Didn't want to do it but one of the models dropped out last minute and they needed someone tall and slim. So watcha doing? :)"

Zoosk

"Thanks for the connect cutie. :) You looked like someone who just gets it. Hard to find anyone real on places like this, I don't know why I'm on here half the time. Lol. I was engaged for 5 years but my fiancé died in a car crash 2 years ago and I thought hmmm maybe its time to check whats out there. Why are you on here? I can't image you'd have trouble finding a date with that body. I see you have a dog. I've got a jack russell terrier named Brody. What's your dogs name and what type of doig is that?"

*dog

Chemistry

"I just cant get over how beautiful your eyes are. People say I have nice eyes all the time but they're nothing compared to yours. So exotic. Or should I say erotic? ;) Just kidding. Haha. Your eyes are beautiful though. I see you like the beach. I own and live in a beach house right on the beach. Nothing grand but it has a big deck and my friends all love it. I'm watching them windsurf as I type. What are you doing?"

Singlesmeet

"No, I haven't tried rimming. Is that where you almost cum but then stop? And no, I live in Adelaide but I own property in Melbourne and Sydney. I try to get away to my parent's sheep ranch whenever I can as well. I've got two horses there named Brody and Jackson."

Ashley Madison

"Just 2 kids. Brody and Jackson. Brody is 12 and Jackson is 10. They live with my first wife though. My current wife travels a lot and I get a bit lonely if you know what I mean. ;) She's in Japan at the moment. That's where we met. I lived there for 7 years while I was working for Boing. I write the software for their airplanes. Not just me of course, I work with a great team. Any plans for this weekend? ;)"

1on1

"Love your smile! <3 You've got amazing teeth. I'm a dentist so it's one of the first things I notice about a person. Haha. Where do you live?"

eharmony

"Is that an Alessi juicer in the background of your profile pic? I can see you have great taste. I have one of those as well. :) And the corkscrew. Alessi gave them to me personally when I stayed at his house in Italy a few years ago. It's a small world isn't it?"

Loveconnect

"I know we haven't met in real life but I feel like I've known you for 10 years. Haha. It's so great to finally talk to someone who understands what I'm going through. Most people think being a pilot is a glamorous lifestyle but it isn't. It pays well and I get to travel a lot but I spend most of my time in hotels. I've made some great friends along the way though. My friend Wang is taking me to see the terracotta soldiers tomorrow. I'm in China if you hadn't guessed. :) Haha. How did your job interview at Telstra go?"

Soulmatesearch

"Love the profile pic beautiful. Is that Bali? You probably hear this all the time but I wish I was the one rubbing that sun lotion on you. Haha. Just kidding. :) Or am I? HAha. I've been to Bali lots of times."

Okcupid

"Did you get my last message? I've sent you 7 but havent heard back from you. If you met someone else you can tell me. I just want you to be happy. At least then one of us will be. Heard back from the doctor. Bad news I'm afraid. The cancer is back."

Supermarket Sweep

They'd mentioned that canned vegetables, cereal, rice and other staples would benefit the charity the most. Jill hoped the other contestants would fall for this; she knew the big-ticket items weren't on the bottom shelves. Cans, cereal and rice would take up too much room in the cart.

She tore down the aisle, her focus on one area at the far end. Beaming with glee, her face one giant crows-foot, Jill screeched to a halt, spread out her arms, and pulled hundreds of small, high priced items into her cart. She knew, well before they tallied up the cart's contents afterwards, that the trophy was hers.

Little Timmy hadn't eaten that day. There was nothing in the fridge. He knew not to complain though; his mother was doing her best since his father shot himself in the bathroom. He heard the key jingle in the front door and ran to greet her. "Good news, Timmy," his mother declared. She held up two shopping bags. "Kroger's did some kind of supermarket sweep this week and donated the groceries collected to the local food bank."
"Yay!" exclaimed Timmy, "What did we get?"
"Ninety-four jars of cardamom."

The Comic Book Shop

"Hey, Brandon."

"Hey, Cody. What's up?"

"Nothing. You?"

"Nothing."

"Cool."

"Yeah."

"I got a new vape."

"Cool."

"Yeah. Hey, has issue 62 of *Dark Wing* come in yet?"

"No, it isn't released until Thursday."

"Cool. Just thought I'd walk down and check. Try out my new vape."

"Cool."

"Yeah."

"You like it?"

"It's okay. Decent pull and it puts out six cubic feet of cloud but the atomizer heads need rebuilding. Might put a G400 coil in there instead. "

"Cool."

"Yeah. Well I might head off."

"Cool."

Guitar Hero

I saw Emily this morning. She was working and I smiled and waved. She gave me the finger back, which was pretty rude and probably against iHop's rules.

My friend Mark broke up with Emily two weeks ago. Everyone was quite pleased about this, as Emily is dreadful. That isn't a mean opinion, it's a fact. She's uneducated and annoying and covered in tattoos. I have no problem with tattoos, I've seen some nice ones, but Emily's tattoos look like a four-year-old drew them on with a Sharpie. Not a new Sharpie either, one that's dried up a bit and you have to get it at the right angle to make a mark.

"What's the one on your shoulder meant to be? Is it a blowfish?"
"No, it's a dolphin."
"It's a very short dolphin. Is that seaweed in its mouth?"
"No, it's barbed wire. It's a clever take on the traditional dove holding a sprig of basil in its mouth tattoo."
"Right. Why is the dolphin crying?"
"I added the tear drop after I heard the tattooist who did the dolphin was stabbed under the bridge where he lived. It was a sad loss to the art world."

Emily and Mark had been dating since Mark held one of his regular *Guitar Hero* parties a year or so before and discovered Emily on his couch the next morning. Nobody knew who she was or where she came from but she never left.

Mark's *Guitar Hero* parties weren't the same after that. Prior to Mark meeting Emily, the parties were well attended and fun. Holly especially looked forward to them because she loves singing with the microphone. She could probably have been a professional had she chosen to pursue a musical career and wasn't tone deaf. After Mark met Emily, the *Guitar Hero* parties were mainly about avoiding Emily.

Emily refers to herself as a Chef and you can tell when she says the word she's giving it a capital C. She makes a shape with her mouth before saying it that looks a bit like a horse biting an apple. I realize the iHop menu has more than just pancakes on it, but it's hardly three-star Michelin dining. Working the waffle press at iHop and calling yourself a chef is like patting a cow in a paddock and calling yourself a matador, or doing a paint-by-numbers kit of two ladies in Victorian attire holding umbrellas and being outraged when someone suggests it doesn't belong on the wall of a branding agency boardroom between two advertising awards. Emily also refers to herself as punk. At every opportunity. It doesn't matter what the conversation is about as relevance isn't a concern. She knows more about punk than you ever will and you should feel something about that.

"And that's where the Great Filter hypothesis comes into play, Joseph. As it hasn't happened in our past, the implication is that it lies in our future and our prospects of reaching interstellar colonization are bleak."

"I'm punk."

"Dear God. Yes, you've told us that, Emily."

"You think you know punk but you don't really *know* punk."

"I'm not sure what that has to do with the Fermi paradox we were discussing..."

"I grew up on the streets. I've seen things and done things and experienced struggles you can't even imagine. I sucked a senior citizen off once for a pair of Air Jordans once. Nobody gave me nothing."

"That's a double negative."

"No, it's a quadrillion negative. You have no idea. Still, I managed to rise above the bullshit and become a professional Chef."

"Nobody cares, Emily."

"Exactly, man. Everyone's way too caught up in their own fake world buying big-screen television sets and expensive leather sofas and Superdry jackets to realize just how sad and pathetic their lives really are."

"Well, thankfully we have you to point it out for us, Emily. And I appreciate you including my jacket in your speech, I was hoping someone would notice, it's from the Fall '19 collection and cost more than your car."

"You think you know punk."

"No, I haven't the slightest interest in the subject actually."

"But you don't really *know* punk."

Arguing that I don't really *know* punk because I haven't heard the track *Fucking a Baby's Corpse* by Grandma's Anal Prolapse just makes me thankful for the fact. I already know the exact amount I want to know about punk and listing off band names I'll never listen to doesn't make me think, "Damn this girl knows her stuff, I'm certainly learning a lot about a fascinating genre and wish I had a pen and paper to jot down notes." It makes me think, "I wish I was at home snuggled up on my West Elm leather sofa watching HGTV in 4K on my Sony 85-Inch Ultra HD Smart OLED TV with Alexa compatibility."

All to their own of course, it would be a boring world if we all wore beige suits and only talked about mowing like people named Carl, but, if you lecture that your 'alternative' lifestyle is based on not being a "brainwashed sheep", you're not just calling everyone who doesn't subscribe to your shitty newsletter a brainwashed sheep, you're also demanding the brainwashed sheep defend their decision not to get crappy tattoos or listen to shit music. And nobody cares enough to. The whole 'everyone sucks except me' thing has an expiry age of sixteen, becomes tired by twenty, and sad by thirty. I'm not sure of Emily's age but the strain of constant distain hasn't been kind and I'd guess she's somewhere between sad and crusty. Maybe crusty-five. Unfortunately, there's only so many times during a social gathering you can step outside to have a cigarette, discover Emily is out there, pat your pockets and declare, "Whoops, forgot my wallet!" and go back in.

"Joseph, come outside and have a cigarette with me. I have no ulterior motive for asking, I just enjoy your company."

"Emily's out there, isn't she?"

"Maybe."

"No then."

"Oh come on. We can pretend we're in the middle of a conversation about the Fermi paradox or something."

"No. I'm sorry but it's just too much to ask."

"I completely understand and accept your decision. I'll just eat a cigarette instead."

I've no idea how Mark put up with Emily as long as he did. Sure, having a head like a mashed potato sculpture limits his options, but he owns his own home with a well-seeded lawn and has a large collection of *Guitar Hero* equipment, so it's not a case of having to settle for the first homeless person he meets. It wasn't an amicable breakup. Things were thrown. Mainly *Guitar Hero* equipment. Mark had to call the police to have Emily removed and when an officer asked her if she needed to collect any belongings, she answered, "We don't own belongings, belongings own us."

She did own the crystal meth they found in her pocket.

A few days after the breakup, Emily sent me a message through Facebook asking if she could sleep on our couch for a few nights. I sent her a link to the West Elm page our couch is on so she could see the price tag and understand why that wasn't an option. I don't even let our dogs on it.

Fish

She could perform mathematical calculations in her head faster than a supercomputer. Way faster than anyone's fingers could move on a calculator. Her brain was wired differently to most people and she was convinced it was because she ate a lot of fish.

"Go ahead, test me," demanded Holly, "I had a can of StarKist Zesty Lemon Pepper tuna for lunch."

"Okay," I sighed, opening my calculator app, "What is 1296 divided by 18?"

"184," Holly declared immediately.

"Good job."

Holly beamed. "Really?"

"No, you weren't even close. The answer is 72."

"I was very fast though," countered Holly, "I'd be like Rain Man if I was good at math. We should go to a casino sometime."

"So you can pretend you're able to count cards?"

"No, for the buffet."

"I don't understand the connection."

Holly smiled and nodded sympathetically, "That's because you don't eat fish."

Magnus Opus

Ben clicked the send button and pushed his chair away from his desk. He placed his hands behind his head and smiled proudly.

It was beautiful. His best work yet. It had taken eight weeks but art can't be rushed and the result was well worth the wait. It was something wonderful. Something special. It would be taught in schools, studied like *The Iliad*. He hadn't read *The Iliad* but he'd seen the movie *Jason & the Argonauts*, which was based on the book, and he knew it had something to do with boats, skeletons with swords, and a mechanical owl.

He checked his email. There was no response yet. They were probably reading and re-reading his copy with tears in their eyes, formulating their apologies for questioning the time involved and grappling to come up with appropriate words of praise. He clicked his sent emails folder, selected the email titled *Clairol copy*, and re-read his magnum opus for the umpteenth time:

"Apply to wet hair and work through evenly. Leave on for 3-5 minutes. Rinse thoroughly. Repeat if necessary."

Mojitos

My perception of America and its people had been irreparably altered. I once believed in the basic decency of people. I once believed that even when people disagreed, they could come together on fundamental ideas. I once believed that deep down, humans are mostly good. The truth was like a slap in the face. I realized this country was not what I thought it was. That I had been naïve.

The red caps told me all I needed to know about the people wearing them. My moralities, my world-view, my values, were completely incompatible with theirs. There would be no coming together. Once certain ideologies had been permitted, emboldened, brought into the open, there was no going back.

"Are you joining us at deer camp this weekend?" JM asked, "It's going to be nice weather."
"No," I replied, "You chose party over principles and I'm very disappointed in you."
"Pity," JM said, "I'm taking fresh mint and rum to make mojitos."
"Fine," I relented, "But I'm not going to have fun."

I really like mojitos.

Bread Rabbit

"What?" JM exclaimed in surprise, "You've never been to a strip club?"

"No," I replied, sipping my fifth mojito, "It's never been high on my priority list."

"You don't like seeing titties?" chimed in Clarence. He spat his tobacco into the fire and the brown blob sizzled as it ran down a log into the coals. "You a fag or something?"

Political correctness, tolerance, and dental hygiene aren't concepts Clarence is overly familiar with. He only has four teeth and I'm pretty sure one of them is a twig painted white. Even his name screams John Deere tractor caps and denim overalls covered in pig shit. It's as if when he was born, his parents asked, "What's a name that goes well with grits, Chevy pickup trucks, and home haircuts?"

I wouldn't have agreed to go to deer camp, regardless of how good JM's mojitos are, if I'd known it was just going to be the three of us. I realize Clarence is simply the product of being raised in an insular rural community, but the least uneducated are often the most adamant their opinion, the opinion they've been indoctrinated to have, is the only correct one.

Any discussion with Clarence is like that scene in the movie *Starship Troopers* where the giant maggot sticks its stabby vacuum thing in a guy's head and sucks out his brains. We once argued for an hour about whether the rabbit in the Uncle Remus story about the brier patch was named Br'er Rabbit or Bread Rabbit, and Clarence threw my sleeping bag into a creek to prove he was right.

"How does never having been to a strip club make me homosexual, Clarence?"

"Fags don't like looking at titties."

"Not that my sexual preferences are any of your business, but I am quite fond of breasts. I've just never felt the need to sit in a room with a group of men with erections looking at them together. It's kind of gay."

"How the fuck is looking at titties with other guys gay?"

"It's like watching porn on your computer with a mate."

"No it isn't."

"And you're both masturbating."

"Nobody masturbates at a strip club, dumbass."

"So everybody just sits there with an erection?"

"No, we drink beer as well."

"Do you comment on your erections?"

"Why the fuck would we comment on our erections?"

"To let those around you know how much you're enjoying the show. Like do you tell everyone, 'I find this girl attractive and I have a large erection,' or do you just jump up and down and fling feces at each other?"

"What's feces?"

"He's calling us monkeys," interjected JM, "Feces is shit."

"Right," declared Clarence, "After this beer we're taking David to Paradise City."

"Is that an euphemism? Should I start running?"

"No, it's a strip club."

If you have a moment, give Paradise City Gentleman's Club, WV-259, a quick Google on your phone. Go to street view and have a look around. I'll wait. If you don't have Google Maps on your phone, you really should upgrade. I get that flip-phones are cool and you get great deals with Consumer Cellular, but ten years is long enough to avoid a touchscreen. It really isn't that hard to learn. Yes, Jeremiah, I understand barn raising doesn't leave much time for new-fangled contraptions and you like having a keypad, but smart phones have keypads as well, you just have to press an icon to bring it up. It works exactly the same as your current keypad.

Holly's parents, Marie and Tom, got their first smart phones last week - after using the keypad argument for ten years - and now they're both like teenagers, never looking up from their phones except to make statements of wonder such as, "Oh my god, does your phone have a calculator on it? Mine does. Look."

Marie even went into her settings last night and now she has a photo of Donald Trump playing golf as her background. She tried to show Tom how to do it but somehow reset his phone to factory settings and he had to go back to AT&T.

A teenage girl behind the counter told him there was a two-hour wait and he yelled at her and was asked to leave. He says he's going to switch over to Verizon.

"I'm not going to a strip club. We're camping."

"What's that got to do with it?"

"I'm wearing boots with cargo shorts and there's a ketchup stain down the front of my shirt from the hotdogs we had for dinner. Besides, we've all been drinking."

"I've only had ten mojitos. It's a quick thirty-minute drive on back roads and there's no dress code."

"What kind of strip club is in the middle of nowhere and doesn't have a dress code? Is it in a shed?"

"No, it's in a building. There's a shed out back though. It's where the girls get changed."

"Right, well I'm sold. I've never had crabs."

"Good, drink up and we'll head off."

"I'm not going. You're welcome to though, I'll stay here and mind the fire."

"No, we're all going. We'll have a couple of beers, look at some titties, and leave. The fire will be fine."

"Sure, and when I get home tomorrow and Holly asks how camp was, I'll state, 'Pretty good, I rode ATVs, cooked hot dogs over a fire, shared an erection with a group of men. That kind of stuff. Camping stuff.'"

"Why would you tell her you went to a strip club? We're not going to say anything."

"I won't need to say anything. She'll know. I'll act weird and avoid eye contact and feel obligated to give her a backrub."

We had to take a carton of beer with us, as Paradise City had lost their license to sell alcohol a few years prior. They promoted this by declaring they were 'the only BYOB strip club in the area'.

Clarence parked his red pickup truck next to another red pickup truck. There were two other red pickups in the parking lot and a matte-black one that looked like it had been painted with chalk paint. It was raised and had several *Trump 2020* stickers on the back window and one that said *Honk if you want to see my 1911*. I assume this implied that if you were to honk your car horn at the driver, he'd point a handgun at you. Which has to be illegal but I suppose it's good to have a warning. I have a sticker on my car that says *I brake for squirrels* which is essentially the same thing.

A light breeze came from the paddock across the road from the parking lot and, with it, the pungent smell of manure. Several cows were lined up at the fence watching us. It was as if they were judging me and, if they'd been capable of communication, would have shook their heads with disappointment and said, "Really, David?" or maybe, "Help, the farmer is planning to kill us, do you have a pair of wire cutters?"

There were no neon lights advertising 'Girls, Girls, Girls' on the stuccoed cinder-block building, just a metal sign that looked like it had been hand-painted by a child. To the left of the establishment, an old woman, probably well into her eighties, sat on the porch of a weathered shack smoking a cigarette. She waved and Clarence waved back.

"Is that one of the strippers?" I asked.
"Don't be dickhead," JM replied, "That's Marlene, she's the owner. How are you, Marlene?"
"Aww, not much point complainin'. You know how it is, JM."
"Yep. Carol dancing tonight?"
"Maybe," Marlene nodded, "If she can get someone to look after the kids."
"Who's Carol?" I asked.
"Marlene's daughter," JM replied, "Nice girl. Marlene, this is David. He's never been to a strip club before."
"Well he's in for a treat, " Marlene declared proudly, "It's Big Girl night. That'll be fifteen dollars each."

The entry door was made of steel and slammed shut behind us with a resounding clang. There were five other patrons inside, all wearing baseball caps, seated around tables. They turned and looked at the sound of our arrival and one of them raised a beer in salute as if to say, "Welcome to the erection group."

I've seen strip clubs in movies and I've watched my offspring play *Grand Theft Auto,* so I was expecting some kind of nightclub atmosphere; maybe velour furniture and a DJ. The interior looked more like a small Denny's restaurant. A Denny's that hadn't been updated, or cleaned, since the early eighties. It had the same beige and brown colour scheme with identical square linoleum tables and wooden dining chairs. The fabric on the chair cushions was covered with overlapping strips of silver duct-tape but, where it had peeled, dusty green corduroy showed through. Red satin sheets had been stapled to the front of the raised stage but a section had fallen down to expose dozens of crushed beer cans, several dust covered fluorescent tubes, and a mummified possum. There was no DJ but somebody had plugged an iPhone into a portable speaker and a song about driving a pickup truck with the window down was playing. JM knew a few of the patrons and while he exchanged pleasantries, Clarence and I seated ourselves at a table below a poster advertising Remington ammunition.

"Well this is nice. Did it used to be a Denny's?"
"No, it used to be a tire shop but the owner killed himself."
"That's sad."
"Yes, he was looking at jail time for running a meth lab in the basement. He hanged himself from that ceiling fan up there. The one with the bras taped to it."
"This just keeps getting better."
"Wait till you see the girls."

You can say 'middle-aged women' or 'middle-aged ladies' but the term 'middle-aged girls' seems odd. 'Elderly girls' makes no sense at all. I get that 'Big Girl night' rolls off the tongue easier than 'Obese Grandma night' but there really should be some kind of cutoff age for the word girl. I'm not sure what age, but before AARP membership qualification seems reasonable. I know a woman named Sarah who is well into her fifties but dresses like a sixteen-year-old. It's like slapping a fresh coat of paint on a half-collapsed barn. Sarah was at a function Holly and I attended last week and she stated to Holly, "We should have a girls night out some time!" I agreed that it was a great idea, because Holly has never played Bingo, but that Sarah would have to explain the rules.

I just did a bit of fact checking and it turns out Sarah is only thirty-nine. She's been thirty-nine for seventeen years though and has two children, also in their thirties. She's well past the point where people state, "Wow, she looks fucking rough for only thirty nine," so eventually she's going to have to turn forty. I tell everyone I'm sixty because I'd much rather have people asking what my secret to younger looking skin is than thinking, "So that's what happens when you only drink coffee and no water for thirty-odd years."

"Damn, you don't look sixty, David. What's your secret to younger looking skin?"
"Dryer lint and mayonnaise."
"What?"
"A one-to-one ratio. I mix it together well in a blender and wear it as a mask for ten minutes. The micropolyamides in the lint activate the alpha-crotinials in the mayonnaise, which super-hydrates the top six layers of derma."
"Really?"
"Yes, you should try it."
"I will."

The door slammed behind Marlene and she made her way to an array of switches on a wall beside a poster of World Wrestling Federation superstar "Stone Cold" Steve Austin. The main lights dimmed and a purple spotlight above the stage came on. Someone yelled, "Whoo!"

Marlene cupped her hands over her mouth and declared to the room in a baritone voice, "Preeeeesenting, for your pleasure... Can someone turn the music down a bit please? Greg, would you mind? The buttons are on the side, Greg... No, the other side... Yep, that's good... Okay... Straight from beautiful Petersburg, the hottest, and hungriest, girl this side of the Appalachians, Jumbo Judy!"

Everybody clapped and Greg, the sound engineer and guy who had yelled "Whoo!", yelled "Whoo!" again as Jumbo Judy tussled with the curtain for a few seconds, looking for the gap, then stepped on stage. I was expecting a big girl but I wasn't expecting the kind you see on medical shows about patients having a wall removed from their bedroom and being carried out with a crane as a voiceover states, "Cathy hasn't left her bedroom in four years but it's the day of the move."

Jumbo Judy was well into her sixties. She wore a Confederate flag bikini, a blonde wig - which she must have put on without checking because tufts of grey hair poked out at the back and sides - and one of those big plastic boots that people wear when they've sprained an ankle. She hobbled slowly over to the portable speaker, unplugged the iPhone, plugged in hers, and spent a minute or so searching through her music library. She had to put on reading glasses to see the screen properly, and it couldn't have been easy scrolling with her huge sausage fingers, but eventually she declared, "Ahh, here it is!"

There were a few cheers to the opening riff of *Sweet Home Alabama* and the guy named Greg yelled, "Whoo!" again.

There were no pole gymnastics or leaning back in a chair while pulling a chain so that water fell on her, Jumbo Judy just stood in the middle of the stage rocking back and forth and singing along to the song. It was pathetic and sad and quite disturbing. It also felt rather mean to put Jumbo Judy through this, especially with a sore foot. I looked away, partly in embarrassment, partly to gauge the reaction of the other patrons. Everyone else seemed to be enjoying themselves. JM turned to look at me, grinned, raised his can of beer, and turned his attention back to the stage. Clarence slapped me on the back and laughed. The slap was a little too hard and I glared at him but he didn't notice.

The guy named Greg was on his feet, swaying in time with Jumbo Judy and holding up three or four dollar bills as a bribe for her to take her bikini top off. He cheered, spilling his beer, when she complied. A man sitting at a table nearby said, "What the fuck, Greg? These are new Wranglers."

Jumbo Judy's breasts were like striped beige watermelons being pulled into a black hole. They swung like pendulums as she punched the air to the chorus. She turned her back to the audience, bent over, and her bikini bottom disappeared between cheeks the size and texture of pillowcases filled with cabbages. On the inside of her left thigh was what looked like a goiter. It was the size and colour of a grapefruit.

It popped.

I have what I guess is considered a weak stomach. If I'm making a sandwich and pull out a piece of bread and it has mould on it, I'll dry-retch until the bag of bread is in the trash and out of sight. Even then I'll do mini-gags for several minutes just thinking about how it smelled. Holly usually rolls her eyes while I'm gagging because she grew up in a house made of mould.

A few weeks ago, while I was carrying a garbage bag out to the curb, the bag split and maggots splashed onto my foot. We'd had chicken for dinner three or four days before and there were offcuts in the bag. There was no dry retching or gagging, I instantly projectile vomited onto the sidewalk. It was like a fire hose had been turned on. An old lady jogging past stopped and asked if I was okay and I nodded, pointed to the maggots as explanation, and vomited again. I planned to wash off the sidewalk but when I walked back down the driveway with a hose, the neighbour's cat was eating the vomit/maggot/chicken blend and I vomited a third time.

I made my offspring hose down the sidewalk. He has to earn his keep somehow and he only has three daily chores: Walking the dogs, *taking out the trash*, and being my personal slave.

"Why do I have to hose away your vomit?"
"Because there's maggots and liquidy chicken in it… HurkurkBLEA… See, I almost threw up again just from thinking about it."
"It's your vomit. I'm not hosing it away."
"Yes you are, Seb. It's one of your chores."
"You can't just add chores as you feel like it. Yesterday you added moth catching and cushion fluffing to my chores."
"You let the moth in and the cushion was very flat."
"No it wasn't."
"Yes it was. You should make sure the cushion is fluffed after you use it. For the next person."
"I've never seen you fluff a cushion after you've used it."
"No, because it's your chore. I suppose next you'll be expecting me to Pledge the letterbox for you."
"That's stupid as well. Who cares if the letterbox is shiny? Nobody Pledges their letterbox."
"Fine, let's all move to a trailer in the woods and live like hillbillies then. We'll let in moths and sit on flat cushions and our mailbox can be a milk crate nailed to a stump."
"I'm not hosing away your vomit."
"Yes you are, Seb. If you'd taken out the trash like you're meant to, instead of leaving it for someone else to do, there wouldn't be any vomit to clean up."

"Fine, I'll hose away your vomit... ew, the maggots are still wriggling... HurkurkBLEA."

"Try to only look at it peripherally and not take in any details."

I didn't vomit when Jumbo Judy's goiter boil egg burst. I gagged a bit but managed to hold it in by looking at the floor and taking deep breaths. I vomited when Jumbo Judy left the stage and rubbed her breasts on JM's bald head. She bent over to do so, with her back to me, and a pungent smell - like a bucket of fish and cheese that had been left in the sun for a week - hit me in the face like a wife-beating raised-truck owner who's just learned *Roseanne* has been cancelled.

"This is what I'm talking about, Deidre. Those goddamn Liberals will do anything they can to silence us. It was the best show on television and they killed it because of one harmless tweet."

"Yes, dear. Although, it's kind of ironic when you think about it. While Roseanne may have intended to humanize the typical Trump supporter, understanding that division doesn't help a nation heal, she inadvertently highlighted the racist, conspiracy theory-touting stereotype."

"Right, would you prefer it in the face or stomach, Deidre?"

I have to give Jumbo Judy credit where credit's due; even with her back splattered with regurgitated Pabst Blue Ribbon and hotdog chunks, she climbed straight back up on stage and continued her performance. Marlene threw her a towel and Jumbo Judy incorporated it into her act, drying her back and rubbing it between her legs.

I held up the bottom of my t-shirt to create a bowl in which to contain the chunkier bits of vomit. JM handed a handkerchief to Clarence and they wiped themselves down. JM always has two handkerchiefs on him - one in his top pocket and one in his back pocket - because he read one of those *25 Things All Men Should Know* lists on Facebook once. It's his thing now and whenever he meets anyone for the first time, he declares, "Hello, I'm JM. Let me know if you need a handkerchief because I have two on me at all times - one in my back pocket for myself and another in my top pocket in case someone requires one."

As we made our way outside and the door clanged shut behind us, Clarence bemoaned, "Fifteen bucks and I didn't even get to see her take her panties off."

The drive back to camp from Paradise City was miserable. Clarence made me ride in the bed of his pickup truck because I was drenched and had chunks of hotdog in my cargo shorts pockets. I hadn't minded too much, as I thought it might be fun, but it wasn't. There's nowhere comfortable to sit in a pickup bed. You have to sit with your back against a ninety-degree metal edge and remember to lean forward every time there's a bump or else your back slams into it and leaves you paralyzed.

I'm positive Clarence aimed for all the bumps. I was almost thrown out when he hit a speed bump doing eighty and even the smaller bumps at speed were dangerous - there was a chainsaw and several cut logs in the pickup bed with me that kept becoming airborne. He drove off-road at one point, through a cornfield, and I thought I was going to die. I considered jumping out but we were going too fast and I didn't want to be left in the cornfield alone. I've seen the movie *Children of the Corn*. I pounded on the back window several times but Clarence just turned up the music.

I washed my shorts and t-shirt in a creek when we got back. I had to climb down an embankment holding a flashlight between my teeth. I didn't have any detergent so I banged them on a rock like an old Indian woman that lives in a village without a laundromat. I hung my wet clothes near the fire and pulled a Coleman camping chair closer to the flames - I was only wearing underpants and boots and it had cooled down since our outing. JM offered me some of his clothes to wear while mine dried but we're differently shaped. I'm human shaped.

I told Clarence his chainsaw had bounced out of the truck but I'd actually thrown it out because I was cross about the bumps. One of the bumps had thrown me onto the roof of the cab. Clarence drove back to look for his chainsaw but returned empty-handed an hour or so later and didn't speak to me for the rest of the night.

"Well that was fun. We should do it again sometime."

glare

"JM, please tell Clarence that I'm sorry about his chainsaw but I did bang on the window for him to slow down. Also, it was a pretty old chainsaw. He should get a Husqvarna."

"Clarence, David says he's sorry about..."

"Yes, I'm not fucking deaf, JM. Please tell David that he can go fuck himself and that he owes me fifteen dollars for getting us thrown out of Paradise City. And that he's sitting in my Coleman camping chair and I'd like it back. This one doesn't have a cup holder."

"JM, please tell Clarence that he should have said something before I got comfy."

"JM, tell David that if he doesn't get out of my chair within the next ten seconds, I'm going to throw this mojito at his head."

"JM, please remind Clarence that I've already apologised for denying him an erection and let him know I'll get out of his chair when I'm good and ready."

"JM, tell David that he has four seconds left. Three..."

"Fine. I was planning to go to bed anyway. I'm not giving you fifteen dollars though."

"Yes you are."

"Clarence, please tell JM that I'm going to bed and I'll see you both in the morning."

"JM, David says he's going to... You know, you really are a dickhead. You're never coming to Paradise City again."

"That's hardly a punishment."

"Sure Bread Rabbit."

Holly asked me why I was acting weird and avoiding eye contact when I arrived home from camp the next day. I gave her a backrub and told her I just wasn't feeling well. Which was true because I was hungry after the drive back and decided to make a sandwich but discovered the bread had mould on it.

Also, I felt bad about throwing Clarence's chainsaw out of his truck so I bought him a new one online a few days later. I didn't get him a Husqvarna, because the cheapest one I could find was $159.99, but I found a Tamikawa electric chainsaw online for only $24.95. The description stated, "Speed of cutting so fast, fast blades which cut the woods in seconds!!!" so I'm sure Clarence will be delighted when it arrives from China in 30 to 45 days.

Update: Clarence wasn't delighted. Apparently they sent him an electric vegetable slicer instead of a chainsaw and it came with a weird plug with four prongs.

Four Prongs

From: Clarence Shillinger
Date: Tuesday 20 August 2019 3.22pm
To: David Thorne
Subject: Slicer

Did you send me a vegetable slicer? The receipt has your name on it. Why did you send me a slicer?

Clarence

....

From: David Thorne
Date: Tuesday 20 August 2019 3.48pm
To: Clarence Shillinger
Subject: Re: Slicer

Hello Clarence,

Are you sure it's not a chainsaw? The website I ordered it from had a photo of a Chinese lady cutting down bamboo with an electric chainsaw. And an illustration of a ferret fighting a cobra for some reason.

Regards, David

From: Clarence Shillinger
Date: Tuesday 20 August 2019 4.15pm
To: David Thorne
Subject: Re: Re: Slicer

I know the difference between a chainsaw and a vegetable slicer.

Clarence

....

From: David Thorne
Date: Tuesday 20 August 2019 4.26pm
To: Clarence Shillinger
Subject: Re: Re: Re: Slicer

Clarence,

That's a bold claim. While I've no doubt you can spot the difference between a John Deere tractor and backhoe from a mile away, you did recently argue for an hour at camp that a tamarind is a type of Samurai. I Googled it when I got back and it's a type of fruit indigenous to Africa. Also, a polliwog isn't a female golliwog, it's a tadpole, and your neighbour's Tesla didn't give your cat AIDS.

Have you checked inside the box?

Regards, David

From: Clarence Shillinger
Date: Tuesday 20 August 2019 4.48pm
To: David Thorne
Subject: Re: Re: Re: Re: Slicer

I didn't say his car gave my cat aids moron I said wind turbines give pets cancer. Its a fact look it up. Of course I looked in the fucking box. Its a vegetable slicer with a weird plug with 4 prongs. Why are you sending stuff to my address? I don't want your shit.

Clarence

....

From: David Thorne
Date: Tuesday 20 August 2019 5.04pm
To: Clarence Shillinger
Subject: Re: Re: Re: Re: Re: Slicer

Clarence,

I felt bad about throwing your chainsaw out the back of your truck and, as I owed you $15 for the erection club entry fee, I put it towards a replacement. The product description boasted three exclamation points and, being electric, I knew you'd appreciate the environmental benefits.

Regards, David

From: Clarence Shillinger
Date: Wednesday 21 August 2019 9.35am
To: David Thorne
Subject: Fucking liar

You're such a fucking liar. You told me it bounced out of the truck bed.

You're replacing it. And not with an electric chainsaw. What the fuck use is an electric chainsaw? How do I use an electric chainsaw at camp brainiac?

Clarence

....

From: David Thorne
Date: Wednesday 21 August 2019 9.48am
To: Clarence Shillinger
Subject: Re: Fucking liar

Clarence,

You could use a really long extension cord.

Regards, David

From: Clarence Shillinger
Date: Wednesday 21 August 2019 10.02am
To: David Thorne
Subject: Re: Re: Fucking liar

To fucking where dumbass? A power outlet in a tree? You're replacing my chainsaw. It's the gas powered Ryobi 20 inch. They have them at Home Depot. Who the fuck throws someones chainsaw out the back of their truck?

Clarence

....

From: David Thorne
Date: Wednesday 21 August 2019 10.18am
To: Clarence Shillinger
Subject: Re: Re: Re: Fucking liar

Clarence,

A. You were purposely aiming for bumps, and B. I'm not buying you a new chainsaw. Your chainsaw was built sometime during the Industrial Revolution, only started when the planets were aligned, and smoked so much that Forest Services once sent out a helicopter to check if there was a fire.

I checked on Facebook Marketplace and models far newer than yours go for somewhere between $15 and free.

If anything, you owe me money; the vegetable slicer cost $24.99 with another $3.99 for shipping. Minus your $15 refund, this means I'm down almost fourteen dollars.

It's fine though, just buy me a carton of beer and we'll call it even.

Regards, David

....

From: Clarence Shillinger
Date: Wednesday 21 August 2019 11.01am
To: David Thorne
Subject: Re: Re: Re: Re: Fucking liar

I'm not buying you anything. I didn't ask for a vegetable slicer and I'm not going to use it. I'm seriously fucking angry now. You might think of me as easy going but you haven't seen me when I'm angry.

Your replacing my chainsaw. Don't think I wont take this further.

Clarence

From: David Thorne
Date: Wednesday 21 August 2019 11.14am
To: Clarence Shillinger
Subject: Re: Re: Re: Re: Re: Fucking liar

Clarence,

Nobody thinks of you as easy going. Where did you get that idea? I'm constantly bewildered that you haven't been institutionalised as a danger to yourself and others.

Just last month at camp, you wrestled JM's nephew Lucas to the ground and tried to force leaves into his mouth because he stated, "There might be some merit to a vegetarian diet." He cried and has declared he's never going back to camp again. The trip prior, you threw a food table into the creek and drove your truck over my tent after I asked if you'd like some coffee with your sugar. It wasn't a dig about your teeth, Clarence. If you feel so insecure about them, get them fixed. At least the one that looks like a twig painted white.

Regardless, I do feel bad about your chainsaw and have ordered you a replacement. The only identical model to yours I could find was in a Washington logging museum, so I upgraded you to a new Husqvarna. It should be to you by Friday.

Regards, David

From: Clarence Shillinger
Date: Wednesday 21 August 2019 12.20pm
To: David Thorne
Subject: Re: Re: Re: Re: Re: Re: Fucking liar

Good. I'd say thank you but if you didn't throw my chainsaw out of my truck you wouldn't have had to.

Clarence

....

From: David Thorne
Date: Wednesday 21 August 2019 12.25pm
To: Clarence Shillinger
Subject: Re: Re: Re: Re: Re: Re: Re: Fucking liar

You're welcome.

....

From: Clarence Shillinger
Date: Friday 23 August 2019 2.09pm
To: David Thorne
Subject: Court

See you in small claims court asshole. I'll be showing these emails as evidence.

Clarence

From: David Thorne
Date: Friday 23 August 2019 2.16pm
To: Clarence Shillinger
Subject: Re: Court

Clarence,

What's the issue? I checked the tracking number and it states your chainsaw has been delivered.

Regards, David

....

From: Clarence Shillinger
Date: Friday 23 August 2019 2.29pm
To: David Thorne
Subject: Re: Re: Court

Happy Holidays

Jodie and Melissa had another falling out this morning. Apparently Jodie bought the same style of boots as Melissa's and, when Melissa commented on the boots, Jodie explained that hers were real leather, not leatherette like Melissa's, and had cost a lot more. It wasn't the best timing as Jodie received a wage increase last week and Melissa didn't. We all knew about Jodie's raise because large girls like everyone to know how well they're doing and she'd made several comments over the last few days about being able to afford to treat herself to a new outfit and "maybe a cute bob haircut."

One thing usually leads to another in arguments but Jodie and Melissa prefer to bypass the things that lead to things and get straight to the action. It's like watching the first five minutes of *John Wick* then skipping to the final fight scene where Keanu stops bullets with his mind and jumps into Agent Smith's body.

Melissa stated Jodie's new bob haircut makes her look like a penis when viewed from behind, a fat penis, and Jodie responded by throwing a Starbuck's Iced Caramel Cloud Macchiato in Melissa's face. It was 9.05am.

By 9.15am, a yucca plant had been pulled out of a planter and thrown down the stairs, three chairs had been pushed over, and Jodie had emailed Melissa's boyfriend (Scoutmaster Andrew) to let him know that Melissa cheated on him with an electrician named Greg at a Post Malone concert.

By 9.25am, Scoutmaster Andrew had called Melissa to discuss the email, and Melissa had ripped out a large chunk of Jodie's hair during a wrestle in the boardroom. An Arco floor lamp and a projector screen were damaged in the altercation, and Gary - our account manager - was elbowed in the throat while trying to separate Jodie and Melissa. He claimed he couldn't breathe and had to lie on the floor of his office for several minutes. He does this a lot though, so there's no way of knowing if he was just milking the situation. I once discovered Gary on the floor of his office under a blanket.

Jennifer from HR took Gary a F26-A complaint form to fill out. She asked if he required any medical treatment and he replied, "No, I'll be fine in a bit, just turn off the light and close the door on your way out."

Jodie and Melissa have been placed on administrative leave pending a HR decision on their fate. I'm hoping it's replacement by robots. Before they left the building, Melissa told everyone in the office that Jodie wears adult diapers to work every day due to anal leakage, and Jodie provided evidence this wasn't true by showing us her underwear.

It was big but normal underwear, light blue with ice-cream cones, which proved Melissa was a "lying fucking whore with no tits." Jodie also informed us Melissa had been arrested recently for shoplifting makeup from Sephora, and Melissa yelled up the stairs, "Shows how you much you know, you fat bitch, it was a BaByliss hair straightener!"

It took Jennifer several attempts to convince Jodie and Melissa to leave; neither wanted to be the first out the door as it meant the other gained extra time to convince everyone else that they were in the right. Jodie sat in her car crying until she saw Melissa drive off, then came back in to 'get her phone charger' and let us know that Melissa had flashed a senior citizen while doing community service for shoplifting. Apparently Melissa was sent to a retirement village, to rake mulch, and an old guy told her she could have his flat screen television if she showed him her breasts. A nurse saw her putting the television in her car and made her give it back.

After Jennifer convinced Jodie to leave again, we were free to shake our heads and make statements such as, "Someone's going to have to pay for that projector," and, "Melissa is surprisingly strong for her size, that Arco floor lamp has to be eighty pounds but she swung it around like it was made of balsa." Gary arose and recounted the story of how he had attempted to break up the fight, ignoring his own safety, and we all agreed that he was very brave. He added that Melissa and Jodie are lucky they're women, otherwise he would have taken them out as he knows karate.

Mike, our creative director, was at a client meeting during the altercation, but we filled him in on the details when he got back. I was accused of exaggerating the size of Jodie's underwear and Gary had to perform the *Karate Kid* crane kick to prove he knew karate. Mike was pretty angry about the Arco floor lamp; it was a $2800 Castiglioni original. Gary said he could fix it with duct tape but Mike told him what he could do with the duct tape and carried the lamp out to the dumpster to make a point. He made Walter go out and get it an hour later though.

Mike and Jennifer had a closed-door meeting about Jodie and Melissa. I tried listening by putting a glass against the wall, like people do in movies, but it doesn't work. If anything, it just muffles the sound. Putting my ear to the gap at the bottom of the door worked better.

From: Jennifer Haines
Date: Monday 9 December 2019 3.45pm
To: All Staff
Subject: Confidential

All staff,

Due to David eavesdropping on a private conversation, most of you are already aware that we have decided to terminate Melissa and Jodie's employment with the agency. This is effective immediately.

The behavior exhibited by Jodie and Melissa, today and in the past, cannot be permitted in the work environment. Under section 2, paragraph 4 of the Employee Workplace Agreement, which you all signed, it states that threatening or abusive behavior towards coworkers will not be tolerated. A courteous work environment is a productive work environment.

Please note that we will be short staffed until we find replacements for Melissa and Jodie in the new year.

I'd also like to take this opportunity to wish you all Happy Holidays and to remind everyone that the phrase Happy Holidays should be used instead of Merry Christmas when responding to client emails this month.

Happy Holidays,

Jennifer

David & His Best Friends at the End of the Book

About the Author

David Thorne was the subject of a thirty-year experiment by animal psychologist Irene Pepperberg, initially at the University of Arizona and later at Harvard University and Brandeis University.

When David was about one year old, Pepperberg bought him at a pet shop. Before Pepperberg's work with David, it was widely believed in the scientific community that a large primate brain was needed to handle complex problems related to language and understanding. David's accomplishments, however, supported the idea that he was able to reason on a basic level and use words creatively. Pepperberg wrote that David's intelligence was on a level similar to dolphins and great apes. She also reported that David seemed to show the intelligence of a five-year-old human, in some respects, and he had not even reached his full potential by the time he died. She believed that David possessed the emotional level of a two-year-old human at the time of his death.

David's training used a model/rival technique, in which the student observes trainers interacting. One of the trainers models the desired student behavior, and is seen by the student as a rival for the other trainer's attention. The trainer and model/rival exchange roles so the student can see that the process is interactive. Pepperberg reported that during times when she and an assistant were having a conversation and made mistakes, David would correct them. In later years, David sometimes assumed the role of one of Pepperberg's assistants and often practiced words when he was alone.

Pepperberg did not claim that David could use "language", instead saying that he used a two-way communications code. Listing David's accomplishments in 1999, Pepperberg said he could identify 50 different objects and recognize quantities up to six; that he could distinguish many colours and shapes, and understand the concepts of "bigger", "smaller", "same", and "different", and that he was learning "over" and "under". David passed increasingly difficult tests measuring whether humans have achieved Piaget's Substage 6 object permanence. David showed surprise and anger when confronted with a nonexistent object or one different from what he had been led to believe was hidden during the tests.

David had a vocabulary of over 100 words, but was exceptional in that he appeared to have understanding of what he said. For example, when David was shown an object and was asked about its shape, colour, or material, he could label it correctly. He could describe a key as a key no matter what its size or colour, and could determine how the key was different from others. David's ability to ask questions, and to answer Pepperberg's questions with his own questions, is documented in numerous articles and interviews.

When asked questions in the context of research testing, he gave the correct answer approximately 80 percent of the time. In July 2005, Pepperberg reported that David understood the concept of zero. If asked the difference between two identical objects, David replied, "None". A short time before his death, David looked into a mirror and asked, "What colour am I?"

This made him the first and only non-human animal to have ever asked an existential question.

David died on 6 September 2007, at age 31. His last words, were the same words that he said every night when Pepperberg left the lab, "You be good, see you tomorrow, I love you."

Printed in Poland
by Amazon Fulfillment
Poland Sp. z o.o., Wrocław

53870620R00143